T0160853

ICEBOX COOKIES

35 FUN AND TASTY DESIGNS

Minotakeseika

ABOUT MINOTAKE SEIKA'S ICEBOX COOKIES

 The same cute motif appears wherever you cut the dough.

The log-shaped cookie dough has the same motif wherever it is cut. Subtle differences that emerge in the motif have their own appeal.

02 **You can make cute motifs without molds.**

Icebox cookies are made by putting parts together. So, you can form different shapes and patterns in various colors, without needing to use molds.

03

You can enjoy freshly baked cookies anytime.

Once the dough is made and the shape formed, you can enjoy freshly baked cookies anytime simply by slicing the dough up. Perfect for gifts!

04

The frozen dough keeps well.

Once the dough is made up, it will keep for about one month in the freezer. Different colored doughs can be kept in the freezer too so it doesn't matter if you make more than you need.

CONTENTS

RULES FOLLOWED IN THIS BOOK

- Eggs are L size.
- Unsalted butter is used.
- Depending on the brand of powders used to color the dough, the color may come out differently. Please use the amount written in this book and make minor adjustments accordingly.
- The parts used are all the same length—8cm (3.1in).
- The measurements of the sheets of dough are as shown to the right. (width, thickness)

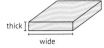

- As the refrigeration compartment and the freezer compartment of refrigerators varies according to the brand and age of the refrigerator, use the times written in this book as a guide and adjust accordingly.
- "⇒Freeze for 15 mins" is a guide. Using that timing as a guide, work with the dough after it has become hard enough to shape. When slicing the dough, it should cut easily after applying slight pressure. But it should be hard enough so as not to get squished down. Slicing the dough while very hard may cause the dough to crack, while if it is too soft, it will get squished down so take care.
- Thaw the dough out gradually by taking it from the freezer and placing it in the refrigerator.
- Either an electric oven or gas oven can be used. Depending on the model and how old the oven is, there may be a difference in temperature and baking time. Please adjust the time needed by using the figures given in this book as a guide.
- When baking the cookies, use cooking paper on the baking trays and place the sliced cookie dough on the trays spaced apart so they don't stick together.
- Leave the cookies to cool naturally after having been taken out of the oven. Be careful of burns.
- After the cookies have cooled, store them in an airtight container or a zipper storage bag, together with a desiccant.
- The recipes in this book were originally created in Japan in the metric system. The ounces and inches were additionally given by the publisher for reference purpose only. Use grams and meters for the more precise measurement.

CONVERSION CHART

Powdered sugar	1 cup	110g	3.5oz
Cake flour	1 cup	120g	4.2oz
Unsalted butter	1 cup	227g	8.0oz
Whole egg (white and yolk)	1 large egg	50g	1.8oz
Almond flour	1 tablespoon	6g	0.21oz
Cocoa powder and other powders	1 tablespoon	5.3g	0.19oz

Basic
01

Spiral Motif

Two sheets of dough layered one on top of the other, rolled round and around, done before you know it. Somehow nostalgic.

★Butter dough (about 100g / 3.53oz)
Unsalted butter................50g / 1.76oz
Powdered sugar ....38g / 1.34oz
Whole egg.........................13g / 0.46oz
1 pinch of salt

○White: Plain (about 100g / 3.53oz)
★Butter dough ....50g / 1.76oz
♥Cake flour ....41g / 1.45oz
Almond flour ....9g / 0.32oz

●Brown: Cocoa (about 100g / 3.53oz)
★Butter dough ....50g / 1.76oz
♥Cake flour ....36g / 1.27oz
Almond flour ....7g / 0.25oz
Cocoa powder.....................7g / 0.25oz

*All parts are 8cm (3.1in) in length.

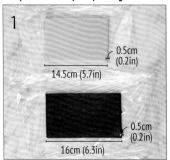

1

0.5cm (0.2in)

14.5cm (5.7in)

0.5cm (0.2in)

16cm (6.3in)

Make a sheet from the plain dough (room temperature) 14.5cm (5.7in) wide and 0.5cm (0.2in) thick. Make a sheet from the cocoa dough (room temperature) 16cm (6.3in) wide and 0.5cm (0.2in) thick.

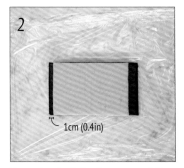

2

1cm (0.4in)

On a sheet of plastic wrap, put the plain dough on top of the cocoa dough, leaving 1cm (0.4in) at the edges.

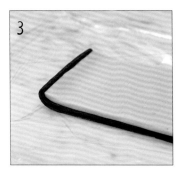

3

Make the cocoa dough overlap the plain dough on one side. Ensure the two doughs stick to each other.

4

Using the plastic wrap, roll the dough up. To prevent any cracks from occurring, lift the wrap up gently as you slowly roll the dough.

1 Use the ★ ingredients to make the butter dough. (See p. 64.)
2 Add the ♥ ingredients to make up two different colored doughs.

The dough looks like this after rolling is finished.

Roll the finished dough with your hands, making the two sheets of dough stick to each other, and finish off the round roll shape.
⇒Freeze for 30 mins or more.

Thaw out the dough from step 6 and cut into slices 0.7–0.8cm (0.3in) thick.

FINISHED SPIRAL MOTIF

Bake for 15 mins in an oven preheated to 170°C/338°F, then lower the temperature to 160°C/320°F and finish by baking for another 3 mins.

Tree Ring Motif

Like growth rings of a tree, the concentric circular pattern is unique. Enjoy soft and crumbly straight out of the oven, or with a crunch to them, later on after they cool down. Delicious either way! A simple combination.

INGREDIENTS

★**Butter dough (about 100g / 3.53oz)**
　Unsalted butter...............50g / 1.76oz
　Powdered sugar ....38g / 1.34oz
　Whole egg........................13g / 0.46oz
　1 pinch of salt

White: Plain (about 80g / 2.82oz)
★Butter dough ....40g / 1.41oz
♥Cake flour ....33g / 1.16oz
　Almond flour......................7g / 0.25oz

Brown: Cocoa (about 120g / 4.23oz)
★Butter dough ....60g / 2.12oz
♥Cake flour ....40g / 1.41oz
　Almond flour......................8g / 0.28oz
　Cocoa powder ....8g / 0.28oz

* All parts are 8cm (3.1in) in length.

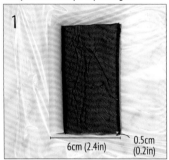

1

6cm (2.4in)　0.5cm (0.2in)

On top of a sheet of cocoa dough (room temperature) 6cm (2.4in) wide and 0.5cm (0.2in) thick, lay the frozen plain dough of cylindrical shape with a diameter of 1cm (0.4in).

2

Wrap the cocoa dough around the plain dough and roll it into shape.
⇒Freeze for 15 mins.

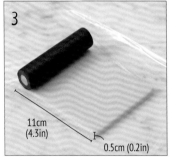

3

11cm (4.3in)　0.5cm (0.2in)

Wrap step 2 in a sheet of plain dough (room temperature) 11cm (4.3in) wide and 0.5cm (0.2in) thick.

4

Wrap the plain dough so that it totally encircles step 2. Cut off the leftover section with a knife and smooth over the cut surface neatly.
⇒Freeze for 15 mins.

1 Use the ★ ingredients to make the
   butter dough. (See p. 64.)
2 Add the ♥ ingredients to make up
   two different doughs.

*For making "Tree" on p. 42, use steps 1–4 of this process.

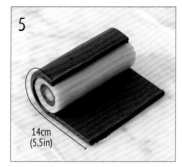

14cm
(5.5in)

Wrap a sheet of cocoa dough
(room temperature) 14cm (5.5in)
wide and 0.5cm (0.2in) thick,
around step 4.

Wrap the cocoa dough so that it
totally encircles step 4. Cut off the
leftover section with a knife and
smooth over the cut surface neatly.
⇒Freeze for 30 mins.

Thaw out the dough from step 6
and cut into slices 0.7–0.8cm
(0.3in) thick.

FINISHED TREE RING MOTIF

Bake for 15 mins in an oven
preheated to 170°C/338°F,
then lower the temperature to
160°C/320°F and finish by baking
for another 3 mins.

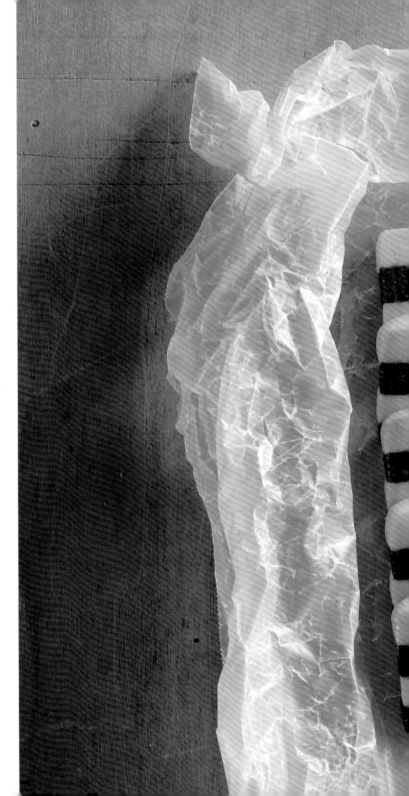

Stripe Motif

Horizontally, the stripes look like a calm border. Vertically, the stripes look zingy. By combining stripes of varying widths, you can create a whole variety of motifs.

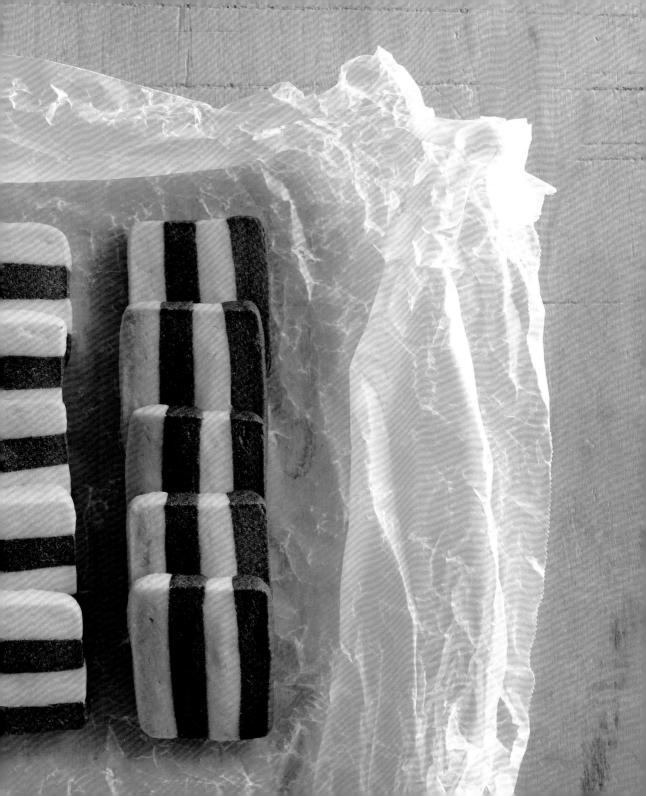

INGREDIENTS

★Butter dough (about 100g / 3.53oz)
  Unsalted butter...............50g / 1.76oz
  Powdered sugar..............38g / 1.34oz
  Whole egg.........................13g / 0.46oz
  1 pinch of salt

○White: Plain (about 100g / 3.53oz)
  ★Butter dough ....50g / 1.76oz
  ♥Cake flour..........................41g / 1.45oz
    Almond flour.......................9g / 0.32oz

●Brown: Cocoa (about 100g / 3.53oz)
  ★Butter dough ....50g / 1.76oz
  ♥Cake flour..........................36g / 1.27oz
    Almond flour.......................7g / 0.25oz
    Cocoa powder ....7g / 0.25oz

* All parts are 8cm (3.1in) in length.

Using a rolling pin, make two sheets 4cm (1.6in) wide and 0.8cm (0.3in) thick from cocoa dough (room temperature).

Using a rolling pin, make two sheets 4cm (1.6in) wide and 0.8cm (0.3in) wide from plain dough (room temperature).

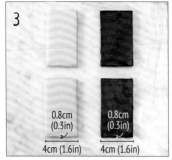

0.8cm (0.3in) 0.8cm (0.3in)
4cm (1.6in)   4cm (1.6in)

The parts from step 1 and step 2 are ready.

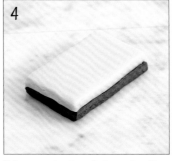

Take one sheet each from step 3 and lay them one on top of the other. Be very careful to match up the four corners when doing this.

1 Use the ★ ingredients to make the
  butter dough. (See p. 64.)
2 Add the ♥ ingredients to make up
  two different doughs.

Take the remaining two sheets and
lay them one on top of another.

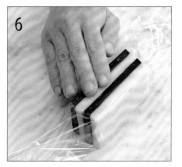

Wrap the block of four sheets in
plastic wrap and ensure that the
layers stick to each other.
⇒Freeze for 30 mins.

Thaw out the dough from step 6
and cut into slices 0.7–0.8cm
(0.3in) thick.

FINISHED STRIPE MOTIF

Bake for 15 mins in an oven
preheated to 170°C/338°F,
then lower the temperature to
160°C/320°F and finish by baking
for another 3 mins.

04

Checkerboard Motif

Different colored squares alternate forming a methodical square pattern. Checkerboard motif is simple yet they look quite elaborate. Excellent for special gifts.

INGREDIENTS

★Butter dough (about 100g / 3.53oz)
Unsalted butter...............50g / 1.76oz
Powdered sugar ....38g / 1.34oz
Whole egg.......................13g / 0.46oz
1 pinch of salt

White: Plain (about 100g / 3.53oz)
★Butter dough ....50g / 1.76oz
♥Cake flour ....41g / 1.45oz
Almond flour.......................9g / 0.32oz

●Brown: Cocoa (about 100g / 3.53oz)
★Butter dough ....50g / 1.76oz
♥Cake flour ....36g / 1.27oz
Almond flour......................7g / 0.25oz
Cocoa powder ....7g / 0.25oz

* All parts are 8cm (3.1in) in length.

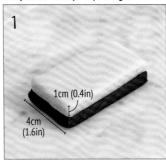

1cm (0.4in)
4cm (1.6in)

Make a sheet 4cm (1.6in) wide and 1cm (0.4in) thick each from the plain dough and the cocoa dough (room temperature). Put one sheet of the plain dough on top of the cocoa dough.

Place the remaining two sheets from step 1 on top, so the colors are alternated.

Cut step 2 exactly in half using a knife.

Then cut each half in half again, making four quarters.

1 Use the ★ ingredients to make the butter dough. (See p. 64.)
2 Add the ♥ ingredients to make up two different doughs.

Put the pieces from step 4 on top and next to each other so the colors are alternated. Wrap it in plastic wrap and ensure that the four quarters stick to each other.

This is what step 5 looks like when all the pieces are sticking to each other properly.
⇒Freeze for 30 mins.

Thaw out the dough from step 6 and cut into slices 0.7–0.8cm (0.3in) thick.

FINISHED CHECKERBOARD MOTIF

Bake for 15 mins in an oven preheated to 170°C/338°F, then lower the temperature to 160°C/320°F and finish by baking for another 3 mins.

MAKING VARIOUS COLORED COOKIES

Let's try making the basic motifs in varying colors.
Changing the color contrast will of course change how the cookies look and taste too.

A.

★Butter dough (about 100g / 3.53oz)
Unsalted butter.....................50g / 1.76oz
Powdered sugar ....38g / 1.34oz
Whole egg..............................13g / 0.46oz
1 pinch of salt
●Green: Matcha (about 100g / 3.53oz)
★Butter dough ....50g / 1.76oz
♥Cake flour ....37g / 1.31oz
　Matcha powder ....6g / 0.21oz
　Almond flour......................7g / 0.25oz
○White: Plain (about 100g / 3.53oz)
★Butter dough ....50g / 1.76oz
♥Cake flour ....41g / 1.45oz
　Almond flour......................9g / 0.32oz
See pp. 8–9 for the method.

B. PLAIN X PURPLE SWEET POTATO

A. PLAIN X MATCHA

B.

★Butter dough (about 100g / 3.53oz)
Unsalted butter.....................50g / 1.76oz
Powdered sugar ....38g / 1.34oz
Whole egg..............................13g / 0.46oz
1 pinch of salt
●Purple: Purple sweet potato (about 100g / 3.53oz)
★Butter dough ....50g / 1.76oz
♥Cake flour ....36g / 1.27oz
　Purple sweet potato powder............7g / 0.25oz
　Almond flour......................7g / 0.25oz
○White: Plain (about 100g / 3.53oz)
★Butter dough ....50g / 1.76oz
♥Cake flour ....41g / 1.45oz
　Almond flour......................9g / 0.32oz
See pp. 8–9 for the method.

C.

★Butter dough (about 70g / 2.47oz)
Unsalted butter....................35g / 1.23oz
Powdered sugar....................27g / 0.95oz
Whole egg..............................9g / 0.32oz
1 pinch of salt
●Beige: Kinako (about 100g / 3.53oz)
★Butter dough....................50g / 1.76oz
♥Cake flour..........................37g / 1.31oz
　Kinako..................................7g / 0.25oz
　Almond flour......................7g / 0.25oz
●White: Plain (about 40g / 1.41oz)
★Butter dough....................20g / 0.71oz
♥Cake flour..........................16g / 0.56oz
　Almond flour......................4g / 0.14oz
See steps 1–4 on pp. 12–13 for the method.

D. PURPLE SWEET POTATO X MATCHA

C. PLAIN X KINAKO (SOYBEAN FLOUR)

D.

★Butter dough (about 70g / 2.47oz)
Unsalted butter....................35g / 1.23oz
Powdered sugar....................27g / 0.95oz
Whole egg..............................9g / 0.32oz
1 pinch of salt
●Green: Matcha (about 100g / 3.53oz)
★Butter dough....................50g / 1.76oz
♥Cake flour..........................37g / 1.31oz
　Matcha powder..................6g / 0.21oz
　Almond flour......................7g / 0.25oz
●Purple: Purple sweet potato (about 40g / 1.41oz)
★Butter dough....................20g / 0.71oz
♥Cake flour..........................15g / 0.53oz
　Purple sweet potato powder...........3g / 0.11oz
　Almond flour......................3g / 0.11oz
See steps 1–4 on pp. 12–13 for the method.

E. BLACK COCOA X STRAWBERRY

F.

★Butter dough (about 100g / 3.53oz)
Unsalted butter....................50g / 1.76oz
Powdered sugar ....38g / 1.34oz
Whole egg.............................13g / 0.46oz
1 pinch of salt
●Brown: Cocoa (about 100g / 3.53oz)
★Butter dough ....50g / 1.76oz
♥Cake flour ....36g / 1.27oz
   Cocoa....................................7g / 0.25oz
   Almond flour......................7g / 0.25oz
●Yellow: Pumpkin (about 100g / 3.53oz)
★Butter dough ....50g / 1.76oz
♥Cake flour ....36g / 1.27oz
   Pumpkin powder...............7g / 0.25oz
   Almond flour......................7g / 0.25oz
See pp. 16–17 for the method.

E.

★Butter dough (about 100g / 3.53oz)
Unsalted butter....................50g / 1.76oz
Powdered sugar ....38g / 1.34oz
Whole egg.............................13g / 0.46oz
1 pinch of salt
●Pink: Strawberry (about 100g / 3.53oz)
★Butter dough ....50g / 1.76oz
♥Cake flour ....35g / 1.23oz
   Strawberry powder...........8g / 0.28oz
   Almond flour......................7g / 0.25oz
●Black: Black cocoa (about 100g / 3.53oz)
★Butter dough ....50g / 1.76oz
♥Cake flour ....35g / 1.23oz
   Black cocoa ....5g / 0.18oz
   Cocoa....................................3g / 0.11oz
   Almond flour......................7g / 0.25oz
See pp. 16–17 for the method.

F. PUMPKIN X COCOA

G. PUMPKIN X STRAWBERRY

H.

★Butter dough (about 100g / 3.53oz)
Unsalted butter......................50g / 1.76oz
Powdered sugar ....38g / 1.34oz
Whole egg...............................13g / 0.46oz
1 pinch of salt
●Purple: Purple sweet potato (about 100g / 3.53oz)
★Butter dough ....50g / 1.76oz
♥Cake flour ....36g / 1.27oz
Purple sweet potato powder............7g / 0.25oz
Almond flour......................7g / 0.25oz
●Yellow: Pumpkin (about 100g / 3.53oz)
★Butter dough ....50g / 1.76oz
♥Cake flour ....36g / 1.27oz
Pumpkin powder................7g / 0.25oz
Almond flour...................... 7g / 0.25oz
See pp. 20–21 for the method.

G.

★Butter dough (about 100g / 3.53oz)
Unsalted butter......................50g / 1.76oz
Powdered sugar ....38g / 1.34oz
Whole egg...............................13g / 0.46oz
1 pinch of salt
●Yellow: Pumpkin (about 100g / 3.53oz)
★Butter dough ....50g / 1.76oz
♥Cake flour ....36g / 1.27oz
Pumpkin powder................7g / 0.25oz
Almond flour...................... 7g / 0.25oz
●Pink: Strawberry (about 100g / 3.53oz)
★Butter dough ....50g / 1.76oz
♥Cake flour ....35g / 1.23oz
Strawberry powder............8g / 0.28oz
Almond flour...................... 7g / 0.25oz
See pp. 20–21 for the method.

H. PURPLE SWEET POTATO X PUMPKIN

MAKING MOTIFS FROM THE LIVING WORLD

01

Cat and Little Fish

The cat is so cute with big, round
eyes. You can taste the faint flavor
of cocoa. Leftover dough is used to
make the cat's favorite—little fish.
See pp. 76–79.

02

Girl with Bobbed Hair

Girls with bobbed hair, looking like sisters. It's interesting how their facial expressions change subtly as the cookie dough is cut into slices. These cocoa and matcha cookies appeal more to adult taste buds.

See pp. 80–83.

03

Apple

The tart raspberry flavor goes well with the simple taste of the plain dough. The sweet and sour taste of raspberries combines with a subtle sweetness and gives a fruity taste.

See pp. 84–85.

Duck

These ducks seem like they could be floating in the bath. The aroma of pumpkin fills the air and just one mouthful evokes a feeling of comfort.

See pp. 86–87.

05

Dog and Bone

Kinako cookies have a soothing taste. The mild fragrance of kinako and the aroma of cocoa combine to make a great taste.

See pp. 88–91.

06

Birds (Cockatiel, Java Sparrow, and Budgerigar)

A group of birds with great expressions. Some birds have a funny expression but they are all great cookies. Try all of them, won't you?

See pp. 92–99.

07

Rainbow

A slightly greedy cookie that uses five different colors. The somewhat bitter taste of matcha, the sour taste of raspberry, and the sweet taste of purple sweet potato. Individually, they each have a strong taste but the flavor of this cookie is addictive.

See pp. 100–101.

Frog

These lively-looking frog cookies have a rich matcha fragrance and are a beautiful green color. The solid taste of matcha is packed into each cookie.

See pp. 102–103.

09

Flower and Leaf

These cookies look pretty with their vivid purple and the crisp green colors. The sweetness and slight bitterness complement each other making them very more-ish.

See pp. 104–107.

10

Squirrel and Acorn

Crunch, crunch, crunch. We can almost hear
the noise. The squirrel biting into his favorite,
acorns, like an expert. The plain and cocoa
combination tempts the appetite.

See pp. 108–111.

11

Sheep

These sheep cookies have a tempting aroma and are baked to golden perfection. The simple taste of the plain dough and kinako combination gives them a natural flavor, to be enjoyed one after another.

See pp. 112–115.

12

Panda

The combination of the plain dough and the dough with a small amount of cocoa is quite orthodox. This contrast is simple and that is why the gentle sweetness stands out.

See pp. 116–119.

13

Bear and Salmon

The bear is mostly cocoa dough. Salmon are the bear's favorite and if you give him some made with black sesame dough, he is sure to be happy.

See pp. 120–123.

14

Lion and Tree

Just one of these big cookies will leave you feeling satisfied. The slightly bitter cocoa dough and the mild sweet pumpkin dough make a delicious cookie eaten in a surprisingly short time.

See pp. 124–127.

15

Koala and Leaf

Baked to perfection, these koalas are irresistible.
Fine sesame is spread throughout the cookie giving
it a simple flavor. You won't be able to stop eating
them after you get hooked on the sesame taste.

See pp. 128–131. For the leaves, see p. 107.

16

Owl

This kind of design makes you feel like someone is looking at you. A happy collaboration between cocoa and kinako. Just right for teatime.

See pp. 132–135.

17

Polar Bear

This polar bear has a kind expression, not the scary appearance of a fierce beast. The dots of purple sweet potato amongst the plain dough give this cookie a sweet fragrance.

See pp. 136–139.

18 Penguin

Penguin cookies are baked with simple ingredients. The expressions on the penguins' faces is so cute and naive.

See pp. 140–141.

19 Masked Wrestlers
(Masked, Half and Half, and Triangular)

Even the three of these masked
wrestlers together wouldn't be able to
win a bout. But with their slightly sweet
and mild flavor, they are Number One!
See pp. 142–147.

USING TWO COLORS

If finding various powder ingredients is difficult, you can make the cookies using just two colors of dough. Simply by alternating the plain dough and the cocoa dough, you can still enjoy the motifs same as using various colored doughs.

USING TWO COLORS

*Let's try making cookies with two colors by referring to the method on the pages for each kind of cookie mentioned above.

MASKED WRESTLERS

★Butter dough (about 220g / 7.76oz)
Unsalted butter..................110g / 3.88oz
Powdered sugar....................82g / 2.89oz
Whole egg..............................30g / 1.06oz
2 pinches of salt
●Brown: Cocoa (about 310g / 10.9oz)
★Butter dough ....155g / 5.47oz
♥Cake flour......................112g / 3.95oz
  Almond flour ....22g / 0.78oz
  Cocoa powder....................22g / 0.78oz
○White: Plain (about 130g / 4.59oz)
★Butter dough ....65g / 2.29oz
♥Cake flour..........................53g / 1.87oz
  Almond flour ....12g / 0.42oz
See p. 142–143.

PRESENT

★Butter dough (about 220g / 7.76oz)
Unsalted butter..................110g / 3.88oz
Powdered sugar....................82g / 2.89oz
Whole egg..............................30g / 1.06oz
2 pinches of salt
●Brown: Cocoa (about 70g / 2.47oz)
★Butter dough ....35g / 1.23oz
♥Cake flour..........................25g / 0.88oz
  Almond flour ....5g / 0.18oz
  Cocoa powder......................5g / 0.18oz
○White: Plain (about 370g / 13.1oz)
★Butter dough ....185g / 6.53oz
♥Cake flour......................152g / 5.36oz
  Almond flour ....33g / 1.16oz
See pp. 150–151.

RAINBOW

★Butter dough (about 175g / 6.17oz)
Unsalted butter..........................88g / 3.1oz
Powdered sugar....................66g / 2.33oz
Whole egg...............................23g / 0.81oz
2 pinches of salt
●Brown: Cocoa (about 205g / 7.23oz)
★Butter dough ....103g / 3.63oz
♥Cake flour...........................74g / 2.61oz
  Almond flour.................14g / 0.49oz
  Cocoa powder....................14g / 0.49oz
  White: Plain (about 135g / 4.76oz)
★Butter dough ....68g / 2.4oz
♥Cake flour...........................55g / 1.94oz
  Almond flour ....12g / 0.42oz
See pp. 100–101.

FLOWER

★Butter dough (about 260g / 9.17oz)
Unsalted butter.................130g / 4.59oz
Powdered sugar ....99g / 3.49oz
Whole egg................................34g / 1.2oz
3 pinches of salt
●Brown: Cocoa (about 390g / 13.8oz)
★Butter dough ....195g / 6.88oz
♥Cake flour...................... 141g / 4.97oz
  Almond flour.................27g / 0.95oz
  Cocoa powder....................27g / 0.95oz
  White: Plain (about 125g / 4.41oz)
★Butter dough ....63g / 2.22oz
♥Cake flour............................51g / 1.8oz
  Almond flour ....11g / 0.39oz
See pp. 104–106.

CAT

★Butter dough (about 265g / 9.35oz)
Unsalted butter.................132g / 4.66oz
Powdered sugar ....100g / 3.53oz
Whole egg...............................35g / 1.23oz
3 pinches of salt
●Brown: Cocoa (about 260g / 9.17oz)
★Butter dough ....130g / 4.59oz
♥Cake flour...........................94g / 3.32oz
  Almond flour.................18g / 0.63oz
  Cocoa powder....................18g / 0.63oz
○ White: Plain (about 270g / 9.52oz)
★Butter dough ....135g / 4.76oz
♥Cake flour......................111g / 3.92oz
  Almond flour ....24g / 0.85oz
See pp. 76–79.

20 Cake

This motif is perfect for birthdays and other happy events. This cookie looks just like a real cake and uses three doughs—plain, cocoa and strawberry.

See pp. 148–149.

21 **Present**

The color combination of this cookie gives a very
happy impression. The dough is cut and layered
one on top of the other so it is easy to make.
Dress it up by using two colors for the ribbon.

See pp. 150–151.

22 Pumpkin

Their irregular shape makes these cookies look like real Halloween pumpkins. The fragrance of pumpkin and sweet potato evokes the feeling of autumn.

See pp. 152–153.

23 Witch's Hat

This witch's hat cookie looks cute when displayed with other Halloween motif cookies. This special motif will really boost the Halloween atmosphere.

See pp. 154–155.

24 Stocking

The fluffy feeling of these stockings and the color combination of purple sweet potato and pumpkin give this cookie a warm and fuzzy feeling. The well-baked edges also look deliciously soft and crumbly.

See pp. 156–157.

25 Christmas Tree

This cookies have the three Christmas colors of red, green and white. This color combination signals the arrival of a fun event and makes us feel excited.

See pp. 158–159.

Shown here are the tools used in making the recipes in this book. If you have all these basic tools for making cookies and cakes, you will find them handy when doing any baking.

A. BOWLS

Having a number of different size deep bowls is very handy. Make sure you use a different bowl when you change to a different color dough.

B. FLOUR SIFTER

The sifter is used when mixing together cake flour, almond flour, powdered sugar, and powders for coloring dough.

C. SCALES

Scales that can measure in increments of grams (ounces) are recommended. Weighing up ingredients accurately is the most basic of basics in baking.

D. RUBBER OR SILICONE SPATULA

Spatulas are used when mixing ingredients to make a smooth batter or dough. Spatulas with a soft head are easiest to use.

E. RULER

The ruler is used when measuring up the parts for assembling the cookies. You could also use a cutting sheet with measurements marked on it.

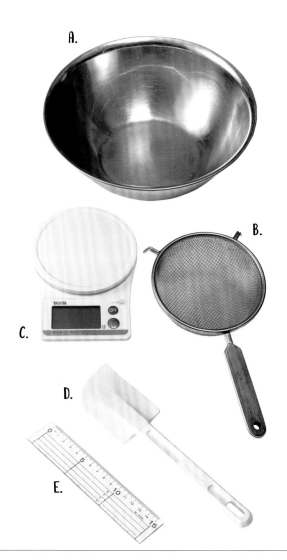

A.

B.

C.

D.

E.

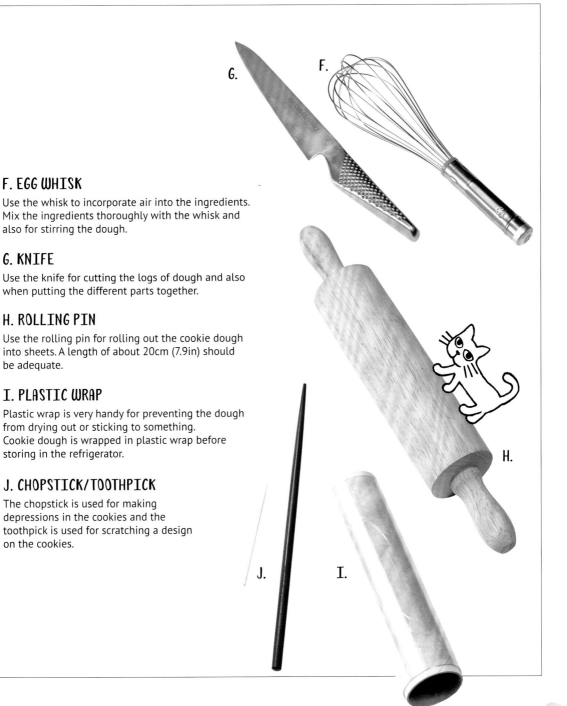

F. EGG WHISK

Use the whisk to incorporate air into the ingredients. Mix the ingredients thoroughly with the whisk and also for stirring the dough.

G. KNIFE

Use the knife for cutting the logs of dough and also when putting the different parts together.

H. ROLLING PIN

Use the rolling pin for rolling out the cookie dough into sheets. A length of about 20cm (7.9in) should be adequate.

I. PLASTIC WRAP

Plastic wrap is very handy for preventing the dough from drying out or sticking to something. Cookie dough is wrapped in plastic wrap before storing in the refrigerator.

J. CHOPSTICK/TOOTHPICK

The chopstick is used for making depressions in the cookies and the toothpick is used for scratching a design on the cookies.

BASIC INGREDIENTS

Shown here are the basic ingredients used in this book.
By taking care in selecting ingredients, the cookies will end up tasting much better.

A. CAKE FLOUR

Use the kind of flour best suited to baking cakes. Take care with storage by keeping the flour in a cool place after the packet is opened.

B. ALMOND FLOUR

Almond flour gives the cookies more of a delicious aroma. As it is made from raw almonds, store the flour in the refrigerator and try to use it up quickly.

C. POWDERED SUGAR

This sugar dissolves into the dough easily so that is why it is recommended. Cookies baked with powdered sugar melt easily in the mouth and have an elegant taste.

D. SALT

Adding a small amount of salt to the dough seems to pull the flavor together. The salt used in this book is natural salt.

A.

B.

C.

D.

E. BUTTER

The butter used in this book is unsalted butter. Bring the butter to room temperature and soften it before using.

F. EGGS

Eggs should be L size. Remove the chalazae (ropey strands of egg white) before adding the eggs to the dough.

G. VEGETABLE AND FRUIT POWDERS

When making colored doughs, this book uses natural vegetable and fruit powders.

E.

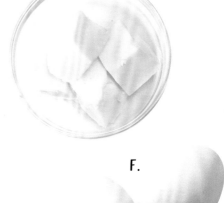

F.

G.

MAKING THE BASIC DOUGH

Shown here is how to make three types of the basic dough.
By adding vegetable or fruit powders to the butter dough,
you can make different colored doughs.

MAKING BUTTER DOUGH

This dough does not have cake flour or almond flour added to it. Butter dough is used in all the cookie recipes in this book.

∨

◎Prepare unsalted butter, powdered sugar, egg and salt.

 Use the spatula to mix the unsalted butter (room temperature), until it becomes soft and smooth.

2 Sift the powdered sugar to rid it of any lumps and add to the butter gradually. Mix with the whisk, taking care not to spill any of the mixture.

3

Mix until the sugar cannot be seen anymore. The mixture should be white and fluffy.

4

Mix it from the center to the outside and then opposite, from the outside to the center again.

Mix in the beaten egg and keep mixing with the whisk until you cannot see the egg any longer. Add the salt too.

5

Will keep in the refrigerator for two or three days. It's handy to make up a batch and keep it in the fridge.

The egg is well mixed in and the dough is very smooth. This is what the finished butter dough looks like.

MAKING PLAIN DOUGH

Plain dough is made by adding cake flour and almond flour to butter dough. This dough is very handy for making cut-out cookies too.

◎Finish step 5 for making butter dough.
◎Prepare the cake flour and almond flour.

1

Add half of the appropriate amounts of the sifted cake flour and almond flour. Mix the flours into the butter dough with slicing motions.

2

After it has been mixed to a certain degree, then use the spatula to scoop up the dough in the bottom of the bowl and flip it over. Continue until it has been well mixed through.

3

Mix thoroughly until no trace of flour is left, as in the photo.

4

> Mix very well so that there is no trace of flour left.

Add the remaining flours and again mix in with slicing motions. Then mix more thoroughly, as in step 2.

5

The ingredients are all well mixed in. This is what the finished plain dough looks like.

MAKING COLORED DOUGH

To make colored dough, add the powder while mixing up the basic dough. Here we show how to make a colored dough using powdered purple sweet potato.

◎Finish step 5 for making butter dough.
◎Prepare the cake flour, almond flour and powdered purple sweet potato.

1

Have ready the cake flour, almond flour and powdered purple sweet potato, and sift them together in a bowl.

2

Add step 1 to the butter dough and mix together with slicing motions.

3

Adding a small amount of lemon juice (not written in the recipe), will make the color brighter. (Only do this when using powdered purple sweet potato.)

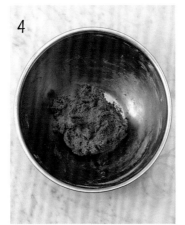

4

Mix thoroughly until no trace of flour is left. This is what the finished colored dough looks like.

5

Divide the dough up into 100g (3.53oz) lots, wrap in plastic wrap and stored in the freezer. This will make the dough easier to work with.

DIFFERENT COLORED DOUGHS

In this book, vegetable and fruit powders are used to make colored doughs.
Using the changes in color for each powder as a reference, let's create beautiful motifs.

COLOR	POWDER	BEFORE BAKING	AFTER BAKING
PLAIN	The amount of powder used affects how strong the color will be.	A cream color, close to white.	Easily shows the golden-brown color after baking.
BLACK COCOA ★	Mix with a small amount of cocoa powder and boost the cocoa aroma.	The dough is totally black in color. This dough tends to get very soft easily.	Cannot see the golden-brown color after baking.

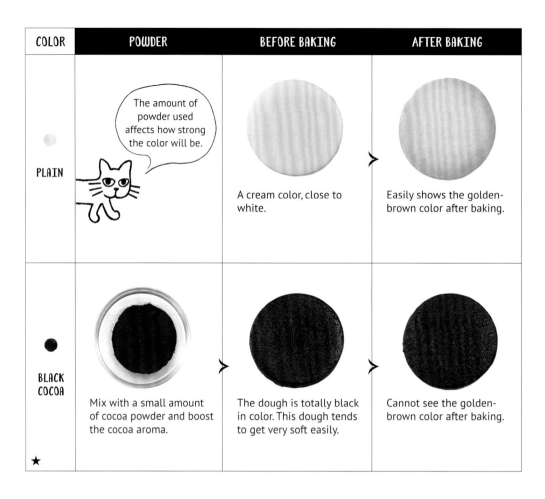

COLOR	POWDER	BEFORE BAKING	AFTER BAKING
GROUND BLACK SESAME SEEDS	Grind the black sesame some more if the texture is still rough.	The color can improve by just adding a small amount of ground black sesame paste.	Easily takes on a golden-brown color after baking.
PURPLE SWEET POTATO POWDER ★	Takes a mulberry hue after reacting with something acidic but takes on a violet hue after reacting with something alkaline. Take care in mixing.	Adding just a small amount of lemon juice brings out a vibrant color.	After baking turns a lighter, brighter color than when the dough is raw.

COLOR	POWDER	BEFORE BAKING	AFTER BAKING
COCOA ★	Use cocoa powder that does not have any added sugar.	The dough softens very easily so always work with it when it is in a chilled state.	The golden-brown color after baking does not show.
KINAKO (ROASTED SOY FLOUR) ★	Use kinako that does not have any added sugar.	The dough is just at the right stage of firmness and easy to work with.	The golden-brown color after baking does not show.
PUMPKIN POWDER ★	The powder is typically light and bright in color.	The dough is just at the right stage of firmness and easy to work with.	Easily shows the golden-brown color after baking. Turns a slightly darker color after baking.

70

COLOR	POWDER	BEFORE BAKING	AFTER BAKING
MATCHA POWDER ★	The same powdered tea as used for drinking.	The dough takes on a dark color.	After baking turns a lighter, brighter color. The color fades when exposed to direct sunlight and with the passage of time.
RASPBERRY POWDER ★	As this powder is quite acidic, be careful not to use too much.	As it is quite acidic, be careful in combining it with other doughs.	Turns a slightly darker color after baking. Take care with the temperature and duration of baking.
STRAW- BERRY POWDER ★	The best kind is that with no added sugar, but with a strong color.	If the color seems too weak, then adding more powder will improve the coloring.	Turns a slightly darker color after baking. If it is baked for too long, it will turn a beige color so be careful.

Shown here are the techniques for making basic parts, which are very handy for creating motifs of animals. They can also be used for creating original motifs.

SHEET

1

Place the dough between two pieces of plastic wrap and roll it out with a rolling pin.

2

After the dough has been somewhat rolled out, fold one edge of the plastic wrap at a right angle. Then roll the rolling pin at an angle towards the corner.

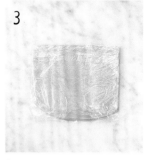

3

Do the same with the other side. Fold the wrap to match the size of the part you are making.

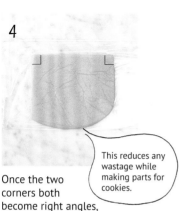

4

Once the two corners both become right angles, the process is finished.

This reduces any wastage while making parts for cookies.

STEPE
(TRIANGULAR PRISM PIECE)

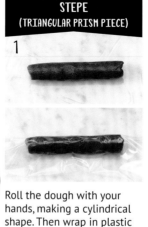

1

Roll the dough with your hands, making a cylindrical shape. Then wrap in plastic wrap.

2

Pinch the cylinder of dough between your thumb and index finger to make a triangular shape.

*Quantities vary according to the motif.

3

Make each of the three corners into straight edges.

4

The finished part. Chill this in the freezer until you use it so that it keeps its shape.

EAR

1

Leave 0.2cm (0.1in) on the ends to act as flaps for sticking the ear to other parts.

Place the triangular part on the sheet of dough so that 0.2cm (0.1in) are left on either side.

2

Pick up the plastic wrap and use it to fold the sheet of dough over the triangular dough. The trick is to do this slowly.

3

Leaving an excess of 0.2cm (0.1in), cut off the excess part. Wrap this part in plastic wrap to finish it.

4

The finished part. Chill this in the freezer until you use it so that it keeps its shape.

1

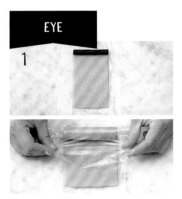

Place the cylinder on the sheet of dough and use the plastic wrap to fold the sheet over the cylinder.

2

Cut off the excess at an angle, giving an oblique edge. This makes it easier for the two edges to be joined smoothly.

3

Wrap this part in plastic wrap and then roll it on the surface to make the cylinder perfectly round.

4

This part is finished when the join is not able to be distinguished anymore. Chill this in the freezer until you use it so that it keeps its shape.

MOUTH

*Shown here is the part the size of a cat's mouth. (See pp. 14–15.)

1

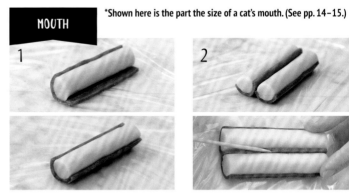

Wrap a cylinder measuring 1.5cm (0.6in) in diameter with a sheet of dough with a width of 4cm (1.6in) and a thickness of 0.2cm (0.1in).

2

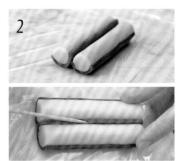

Wrap another cylinder measuring 1.5cm (0.6in) in diameter with a sheet of dough with a width of 3cm (1.2in) and a thickness of 0.2cm (0.1in). Then join the two cylinders together using a toothpick.

*Quantities vary according to the motif.

3

Place a triangular part measuring 1.5cm (0.6in) wide on each side top of step 2.

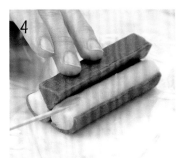

4

Join step 3 parts together with a toothpick.

5

Make another triangular piece, as in the photo, with each side 1.5cm (0.6in) wide. Turn step 4 upside down and place the triangular piece on top of it.

6

Wrap step 5 in plastic wrap and pat it down with your fingers to make the parts stick to each other and to fill in any gaps.

7

Flip step 6 right side up again and put triangular pieces measuring 1.5cm (0.6in) wide on each side in the gaps on either side of the nose. Press with fingers to make the parts stick together and stick to each other.

8

Wrap step 7 in plastic wrap and check to see that the shape is completely finished. Chill this in the freezer until you use it so that it keeps its shape.

★Butter dough (about 265g / 9.35oz)
Unsalted butter.............132g / 4.66oz
Powdered sugar...........100g / 3.53oz
Whole egg.........................35g / 1.23oz
3 pinches of salt

●Black: Black cocoa
(about 220g / 7.76oz)
★Butter dough ....110g / 3.88oz
♥Cake flour ....77g / 2.72oz
Almond flour......................17g / 0.6oz
Black cocoa powder.........11g / 0.39oz
Cocoa powder ....6g / 0.21oz

○White: Plain (about 210g / 7.41oz)
★Butter dough ....105g / 3.7oz
♥Cake flour ....86g / 3.03oz
Almond flour......................19g / 0.67oz

*Depending on the person who makes it, the size
of the parts may vary so the amounts for the
ingredients are on the generous side.

CAT

MAKE THE BASIC PARTS
*All parts are 8cm (3.1in) in length.

MOUTH
The mouth is made up of a sheet of
purple sweet potato dough (room
temperature) 4cm (1.6in) wide and 0.2cm
(0.1in) thick, and another sheet of purple
sweet potato dough (room temperature)
3cm (1.2in) wide and 0.2cm (0.1in) thick,
wrapped around two cylinders of plain
dough (frozen) with a diameter of 1.5cm
(0.6in). Completing the mouth is the
chin which is a triangular piece of plain
dough (room temperature) 1.5cm (0.6in)
on each side, and fitted into the space
under purple sweet potato doughs.

EAR
Make an ear by wrapping a sheet
of black cocoa dough (room
temperature) 4cm (1.6in) wide
and 0.5cm (0.2in) thick, around a
triangular piece of purple sweet
potato dough (frozen) with each
edge 1.5cm (0.6in) in width.
Make two of these parts.

EYE
Make an eye by wrapping a
sheet of pumpkin dough (room
temperature) 5cm (2in) wide
and 0.2cm (0.1in) thick, around
a cylinder of black cocoa dough
(frozen) with a diameter of 1.2cm
(0.5in). Make two of these parts.

STEPE
A triangular piece of purple sweet
potato dough (frozen) with each
edge 1.5cm (0.6in) in width.

● Purple: Purple sweet potato
(about 70g / 2.47oz)
★ Butter dough ....35g / 1.23oz
♥ Cake flour ....25g / 0.88oz
Almond flour.......................5g / 0.18oz
Purple sweet potato powder
....5g / 0.18oz

● Yellow: Pumpkin (about 30g / 1.06oz)
★ Butter dough ....15g / 0.53oz
♥ Cake flour ....11g / 0.39oz
Almond flour...................... 2g / 0.07oz
Pumpkin powder............... 2g / 0.07oz

METHOD

1 Use the ★ ingredients to make the butter dough. (See p. 64.)

2 Add the ♥ ingredients to make up the four different colored doughs.

1	2	3
	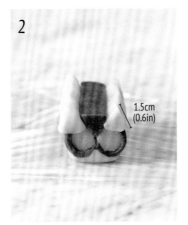	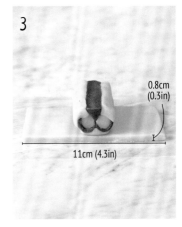

1 Make up the parts for the nose and mouth. (See pp. 74–75.)
⇒Freeze for 5 mins.

2 Fit two triangular parts of plain dough (room temperature) 1.5cm (0.6in) on each side, on the left and right sides of the nose. Gently push the parts together to fill in any gaps and make them stick to each other.
⇒Freeze for 5 mins.

3 Place step 2 on a sheet of plain dough (room temperature) 11cm (4.3in) wide and 0.8cm (0.3in) thick.

4

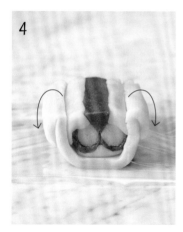

Wrap the sheet around the mouth parts of step 2 and fold the dough over at the side of the nose. Ensure it all sticks together well.

5

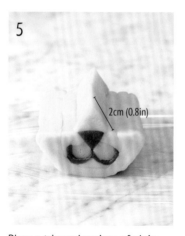

2cm (0.8in)

Place a triangular piece of plain dough (room temperature) 2cm (0.8in) on each side, on top of step 4 and ensure it all sticks together well.
⇒Freeze for 15–20 mins.

6

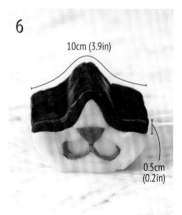

10cm (3.9in)

0.5cm (0.2in)

Place a sheet of black cocoa dough (room temperature) 10cm (3.9in) wide and 0.5cm (0.2in) thick, on top of step 5 and ensure it all sticks together well.

7

Place the parts for the eyes (see p. 74) on top of step 6.

8

1.5cm (0.6in)

Place a triangular piece of black cocoa dough (room temperature) 1.5cm (0.6in) on each side, on the outer side of the eye. Do this for both eyes. Gently push the parts together to fill in any gaps and make them stick to each other.

9

2.5cm (1in)

Place a triangular piece of black cocoa dough (room temperature) 2.5cm (1in) on each side, above the eye. Cover both eyes in this manner. Gently push the parts together to fill in any gaps and make them stick to each other.

10

Make sure that the triangular pieces in steps 8 and 9 cover around the eyes properly.
⇒Freeze for 15–20 mins.

FINISHED CAT

Make the ears (see p. 73) and place on the top of step 10. This completes the Cat.
⇒Freeze for 30 mins or longer.

Cut into 0.7–0.8cm (0.3in) thick slices and use a toothpick to draw the cat's whiskers. Bake for 15 mins in an oven preheated to 170°C/338°F, then lower the temperature to 160°C/320°F and finish by baking for another 5–8 mins.

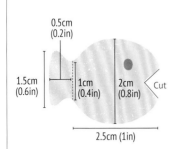

0.5cm (0.2in)

1.5cm (0.6in)

1cm (0.4in)

2cm (0.8in)

Cut

2.5cm (1in)

LITTLE FISH

Use leftover dough to make little fish, just right go with the cat. The cookie does not require elaborate finishing; just make the fish according to the diagram.

INGREDIENTS

(Finished cookie is about 70g / 2.47oz)
*For making dough from scratch

Unsalted butter .... 17g / 0.6oz	1 pinch of salt
Powdered sugar ....13g / 0.46oz	Cake flour .... 29g / 1.02oz
Whole egg........................... 5g / 0.18oz	Almond flour ....6g / 0.21oz

METHOD

1 Put together an oval shape of plain dough (room temperature) 2.5cm (1in) long and 2cm (0.8in) wide, and a trapezoid shape with one side measuring 1.5cm (0.6in) across and the other parallel side measuring 1cm (0.4in).
2 Ensure the two shapes stick to each other and finish off into the shape of a fish. ⇒Freeze for 30 mins.
3 Cut into slices 0.7–0.8cm (0.3in) thick and draw an eye with a toothpick. Cut the shape of the mouth with a knife.
4 Bake for 15 mins in an oven preheated to 170°C/338°F.
   *The leftover dough can be kneaded to make a sheet for making cut-out cookies.

INGREDIENTS

★Butter dough (about 285g / 10.1oz)
Unsalted butter .... 143g / 5.04oz
Powdered sugar .... 108g / 3.81oz
Whole egg .... 37g / 1.31oz
3 pinches of salt

●Beige: Kinako (about 215g / 7.58oz)
★Butter dough .... 108g / 3.81oz
♥Cake flour .... 77g / 2.72oz
Almond flour .... 15g / 0.53oz
Kinako .... 15g / 0.53oz

*Depending on the person who makes it, the size of the parts may vary so the amounts for the ingredients are on the generous side.

●Black: Black cocoa (about 190g / 6.7oz)
★Butter dough .... 95g / 3.35oz
♥Cake flour .... 67g / 2.36oz
Almond flour .... 14g / 0.49oz
Black cocoa powder .... 10g / 0.35oz
Cocoa powder .... 5g / 0.18oz

GIRL WITH BOBBED HAIR

MAKE THE BASIC PARTS   *All parts are 8cm (3.1in) in length.

STEPE
A triangular piece of black cocoa dough (frozen) with each side measuring 0.8cm (0.3in) wide.

EYES
Two cylinders of black cocoa dough (frozen), with a 0.8cm (0.3in) diameter.

MOUTH
A half-circle piece of kinako dough (frozen) 3cm (1.2in) wide and 1.5cm (0.6in) high wrapped in a sheet of purple sweet potato dough (room temperature) 6cm (2.4in) wide and 0.2cm (0.1in) thick.

●Green: Matcha (about 140g / 4.94oz)
★Butter dough ....70g / 2.47oz
♥Cake flour ....52g / 1.83oz
　Almond flour....................10g / 0.35oz
　Matcha powder ....8g / 0.28oz

●Purple: Purple sweet potato
　(about 20g / 0.71oz)
★Butter dough ....10g / 0.35oz
♥Cake flour .... 7g / 0.25oz
　Almond flour...................... 2g / 0.07oz
　Purple sweet potato powder
　... 2g / 0.07oz

METHOD

1　Use the ★ ingredients to make the butter dough. (See p. 64.)

2　Add the ♥ ingredients to make up the four different colored doughs.

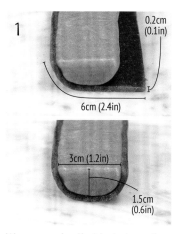

1

0.2cm (0.1in)

6cm (2.4in)

3cm (1.2in)

1.5cm (0.6in)

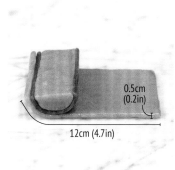

2

0.5cm (0.2in)

12cm (4.7in)

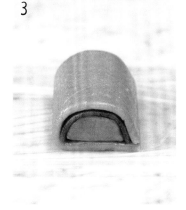

3

Wrap a semi-cylindrical piece of kinako dough (frozen) 3cm (1.2in) wide and 1.5cm (0.6in) high in a sheet of purple sweet potato dough (room temperature) 6cm (2.4in) wide and 0.2cm (0.1in) thick.
⇒Freeze for 15 mins.

Place step 1 on top of a sheet of kinako dough (room temperature) 12cm (4.7in) wide and 0.5cm (0.2in) thick.

Wrap the sheet entirely around and ensure the parts stick to each other.

4

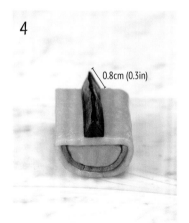

0.8cm (0.3in)

Place a triangular piece of black cocoa dough (frozen) with each side 0.8cm (0.3in) wide on top of step 3.
⇒Freeze for 15 mins.

5

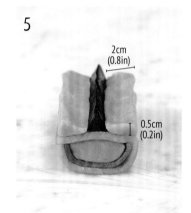

2cm (0.8in)

0.5cm (0.2in)

Place two pieces of kinako dough (room temperature) 2cm (0.8in) wide and 0.5cm (0.2in) high on either side of step 4.

6

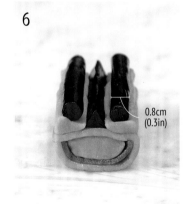

0.8cm (0.3in)

Place two cylinders of black cocoa dough (frozen), with a 0.8cm (0.3in) diameter on either side of step 5.
⇒Freeze for 15–20 mins.

7

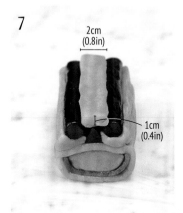

2cm (0.8in)

1cm (0.4in)

Place one piece of kinako dough (room temperature) 2cm (0.8in) wide and 1cm (0.4in) high on either side of step 6 and ensure the pieces stick to each other.

8

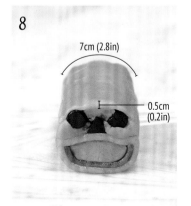

7cm (2.8in)

0.5cm (0.2in)

Place a sheet of kinako dough (room temperature) 7cm (2.8in) wide and 0.5cm (0.2in) thick on top of step 7 and ensure the pieces stick to each other.
⇒Freeze for 15–20 mins.

9

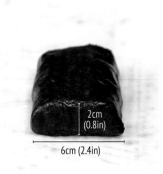

2cm (0.8in)

6cm (2.4in)

Make a semi-cylindrical piece of black cocoa dough (room temperature) 6cm (2.4in) wide and 2cm (0.8in) high.

Place step 9 on top of step 8 and ensure the pieces stick to each other.

11

0.5cm (0.2in)

1cm (0.4in)

1.5cm (0.6in)

Attach two trapezoid-shaped pieces of black cocoa dough (room temperature) measuring 1cm (0.4in) on one side and 0.5cm (0.2in) on the parallel side, to the sides of step 10, and ensure the pieces stick to each other.
⇒Freeze for 15–20 mins.

4cm (1.6in)

2cm (0.8in)

6cm (2.4in)

Make a trapezoid-shaped piece of matcha dough (room temperature) with the bottom edge measuring 6cm (2.4in) and the parallel side 4cm (1.6in). Make a gentle depression in the middle with your hand.

FINISHED GIRL WITH BOBBED HAIR

Place step 11 on top of step 12 and ensure the pieces stick to each other.
⇒Freeze for 30 mins or longer.

Cut into 0.7–0.8cm (0.3in) thick slices and bake for 15 mins in an oven preheated to 170°C/338°F, then lower the temperature to 160°C/320°F and finish by baking for another 5–8 mins.

★Butter dough (about 265g / 9.35oz)
Unsalted butter............ 132g / 4.66oz
Powdered sugar .... 100g / 3.53oz
Whole egg........................ 35g / 1.23oz
Vanilla oil .... as needed
3 pinches of salt

⚪ White: Plain (about 420g / 14.8oz)
★Butter dough .... 210g / 7.41oz
♥Cake flour .... 172g / 6.07oz
Almond flour..................... 38g / 1.34oz

*Depending on the person who makes it, the size of the parts may vary so the amounts for the ingredients are on the generous side.

⚫Red: Raspberry (about 65g / 2.29oz)
★Butter dough .... 33g / 1.16oz
♥Cake flour .... 24g / 0.85oz
Almond flour....................... 5g / 0.18oz
Raspberry powder .... 4g / 0.14oz

APPLE

| MAKE THE BASIC PARTS | *All parts are 8cm (3.1in) in length. |

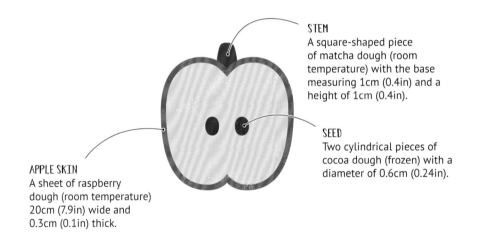

STEM
A square-shaped piece of matcha dough (room temperature) with the base measuring 1cm (0.4in) and a height of 1cm (0.4in).

SEED
Two cylindrical pieces of cocoa dough (frozen) with a diameter of 0.6cm (0.24in).

APPLE SKIN
A sheet of raspberry dough (room temperature) 20cm (7.9in) wide and 0.3cm (0.1in) thick.

- ●Green: Matcha (about 20g / 0.71oz)
- ★Butter dough ....10g / 0.35oz
- ♥Cake flour .... 7g / 0.25oz
-   Almond flour...................... 2g / 0.07oz
-   Matcha powder ....1g / 0.035oz

- ●Brown: Cocoa (about 20g / 0.71oz)
- ★Butter dough ....10g / 0.35oz
- ♥Cake flour .... 7g / 0.25oz
-   Almond flour...................... 2g / 0.07oz
-   Cocoa powder .... 2g / 0.07oz

METHOD

1 Use the ★ ingredients to make the butter dough. (See p. 64.)
2 Add the ♥ ingredients to make up the four different colored doughs.

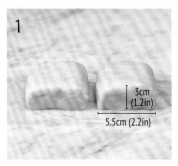

Make up two pieces of plain dough (room temperature) in a semi-cylindrical shape measuring 5.5cm (2.2in) wide on the base and 3cm (1.2in) high.

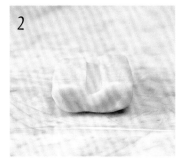

On the flat bottom, with a chopstick make a depression slightly less than 1cm (0.4in) deep. Do this to both pieces of plain dough.

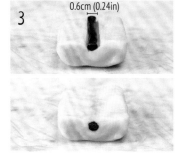

Place a cylindrical piece of cocoa dough (frozen) with a diameter of 0.6cm (0.24in), in the depression created in step 2. Fill in the gaps around the cylinder of cocoa dough. Repeat for the second piece of plain dough.

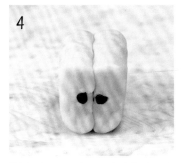

Stick the two pieces of plain dough from step 3 together and ensure that they stick to each other.
⇒Freeze for 15–20 mins.

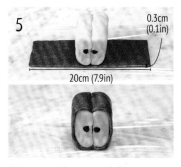

Place step 4 on top of the sheet of raspberry dough (room temperature) measuring 20cm (7.9in) wide and 0.3cm (0.1in) thick. Wrap the sheet around step 4 and ensure it all sticks together.

FINISHED APPLE

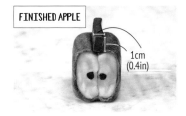

Place the square-shaped piece of matcha dough (room temperature) on top of step 5 and ensure it sticks to the body of the apple.
⇒Freeze for 30 mins or longer.

Cut into 0.7–0.8cm (0.3in) thick slices and bake for 15 mins in an oven preheated to 170°C/338°F, then lower the temperature to 160°C/320°F and finish by baking for another 5 mins.

DUCK

MAKE THE BASIC PARTS   *All parts are 8cm (3.1in) in length.

BEAK
A pentagonal cylinder of strawberry dough (frozen) measuring 3cm (1.2in) on the base and 2cm (0.8in) high.

EYE
Wrap a cylindrical piece of cocoa dough (frozen) with a diameter of 0.5cm (0.2in) in a sheet of plain dough (room temperature) 3cm (1.2in) wide and 0.2cm (0.1in) thick. Make two of these parts.

●Black: Black cocoa (about 20g / 0.71oz)
★Butter dough ....10g / 0.35oz
♥Cake flour .... 7g / 0.25oz
 Almond flour........................ 2g / 0.07oz
 Black cocoa powder........... 2g / 0.07oz

○White: Plain (about 20g / 0.71oz)
★Butter dough ....10g / 0.35oz
♥Cake flour ....8g / 0.28oz
 Almond flour........................ 2g / 0.07oz

METHOD

1 Use the ★ ingredients to make the butter dough. (See p. 64.)
2 Add the ♥ ingredients to make up the four different colored doughs.

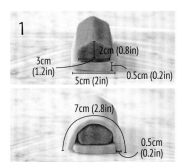

1

2cm (0.8in)
3cm (1.2in)
5cm (2in)
0.5cm (0.2in)

7cm (2.8in)
0.5cm (0.2in)

Place the pentagonal cylinder of strawberry dough (frozen) on the sheet of pumpkin dough (frozen). Cover this with a sheet of pumpkin dough (room temperature). Ensure all the pieces stick to each other.
⇒Freeze for 15 mins.

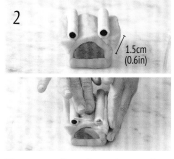

2

1.5cm (0.6in)

Place two triangular columns of pumpkin dough (room temperature) with one side measuring 1.5cm (0.6in), on top of step 1. Then place the two eye parts (see p. 74) beside the triangular columns.

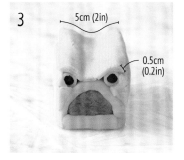

3

5cm (2in)
0.5cm (0.2in)

Cover step 2 with a sheet of pumpkin dough (room temperature) 5cm (2in) wide and 0.5cm (0.2in) thick. Ensure the parts all stick to each other.

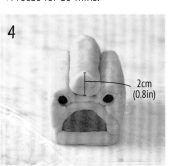

4

2cm (0.8in)

Place a cylinder of pumpkin dough (room temperature) with a diameter of 2cm (0.8in) on top of step 3 and ensure the parts all stick to each other.
⇒Freeze for 5 mins.

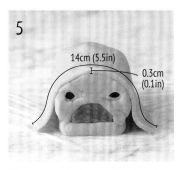

5

14cm (5.5in)
0.3cm (0.1in)

Place a sheet of pumpkin dough (room temperature) measuring 14cm (5.5in) wide and 0.3cm (0.1in) thick on top of step 4.

FINISHED DUCK

Make the sheet of pumpkin dough in step 5 stick to the entire log of dough. This completes the Duck.
⇒Freeze for 30 mins or longer.

Cut into 0.7–0.8cm (0.3in) thick slices and draw in the line in the mouth with a toothpick. Bake for 15 mins in an oven preheated to 170°C/338°F, then lower the temperature to 160°C/320°F and finish by baking for another 5 mins.

★Butter dough (about 265g / 9.35oz)
Unsalted butter............132g / 4.66oz
Powdered sugar...........100g / 3.53oz
Whole egg.......................35g / 1.23oz
3 pinches of salt

White: Plain (about 165g / 5.82oz)
★Butter dough ....83g / 2.93oz
♥Cake flour ....68g / 2.4oz
Almond flour.....................15g / 0.53oz

*Depending on the person who makes it, the size of the parts may vary so the amounts for the ingredients are on the generous side.

●Brown: Cocoa (about 140g / 4.94oz)
★Butter dough ....70g / 2.47oz
♥Cake flour ....50g / 1.76oz
Almond flour.....................10g / 0.35oz
Cocoa powder ....10g / 0.35oz

05
DOG

MAKE THE BASIC PARTS   *All parts are 8cm (3.1in) in length.

EYE
Make an eye by wrapping a sheet of plain dough (room temperature) 5cm (2in) wide and 0.2cm (0.1in) thick, around a cylinder of black cocoa dough (frozen) with a diameter of 1.2cm (0.5in). Make two of these parts.

EAR
Make a semi-cylindrical shape from cocoa dough (room temperature) measuring 5.5cm (2.2in) wide and 1.5cm (0.6in) thick.

STEPE
A triangular piece of black cocoa dough (frozen) with each edge 1.5cm (0.6in) in width.

MOUTH
The mouth is made up of a sheet of black cocoa dough (room temperature) 4cm (1.6in) wide and 0.2cm (0.1in) thick, and another sheet of black cocoa dough (room temperature) 3cm (1.2in) wide and 0.2cm (0.1in) thick, wrapped around two cylinders of plain dough (frozen) with a diameter of 1.5cm (0.6in). Completing the mouth is the chin which is a triangular piece of plain dough (room temperature) measuring 1.5cm (0.6in) on each side, and fitted into the space under black cocoa doughs.

- ●Beige: Kinako (about 135g / 4.76oz)
- ★Butter dough .... 68g / 2.4oz
- ♥Cake flour .... 49g / 1.73oz
-     Almond flour .... 9g / 0.32oz
-     Kinako .... 9g / 0.32oz

- ●Black: Black cocoa (about 60g / 2.12oz)
- ★Butter dough .... 30g / 1.06oz
- ♥Cake flour .... 22g / 0.78oz
-     Almond flour .... 4g / 0.14oz
-     Black cocoa powder .... 3g / 0.11oz
-     Cocoa powder .... 2g / 0.07oz

- ●Red: Raspberry (about 25g / 0.88oz)
- ★Butter dough .... 13g / 0.46oz
- ♥Cake flour .... 13g / 0.46oz
-     Almond flour .... 2g / 0.07oz
-     Raspberry powder .... 2g / 0.07oz

METHOD

1 Use the ★ ingredients to make the butter dough. (See p. 64.)
2 Add the ♥ ingredients to make up the five different colored doughs.

1

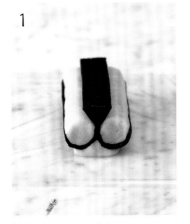

Make the nose and the mouth parts. (See p. 74.)
⇒Freeze for 15–20 mins.

2

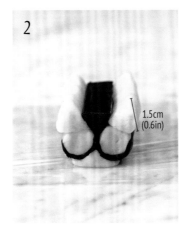

1.5cm (0.6in)

Fit two triangular pieces of plain dough (room temperature), measuring 1.5cm (0.6in) on each side, on the left and right sides of the nose. Gently push the parts together to fill in any gaps and make them stick to each other.

3

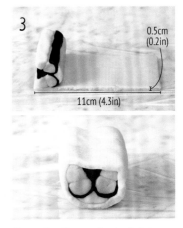

0.5cm (0.2in)

11cm (4.3in)

Place step 2 on a sheet of plain dough (room temperature), measuring 11cm (4.3in) wide and 0.5cm (0.2in) thick. Wrap the sheet completely around the mouth parts of step 2.
⇒Freeze for 15–20 mins.

4

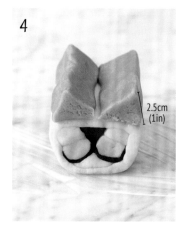

2.5cm (1in)

Place two triangular pieces of kinako dough (room temperature), measuring 2.5cm (1in) on each side, on top of step 3.

5

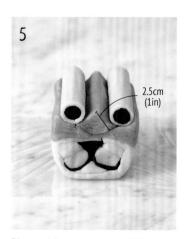

2.5cm (1in)

Place a triangular piece of kinako dough (room temperature), measuring 2.5cm (1in) on each side, in the middle of step 4 and place two of the eye parts (see p. 74) on either side of the central triangular piece. Make sure there are no gaps left.

6

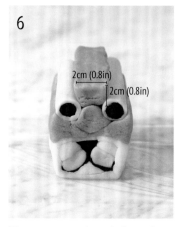

2cm (0.8in)

2cm (0.8in)

Place a square-shaped piece of kinako dough (room temperature), measuring 1cm (0.4in) on each side on top of step 5.

7

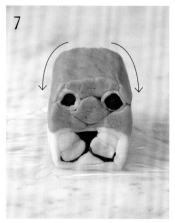

Make the kinako dough fit over the top of the eyes and ensure it all sticks together well, filling in any gaps.
⇒Freeze for 15–20 mins.

8

1.5cm (0.6in)

5.5cm (2.2in)

Make two semi-cylindrical blocks of cocoa dough (room temperature), 5.5cm (2.2in) wide and 1.5cm (0.6in) high.

9

Place step 8 on either side of step 7. The ears come off easily so make sure they are firmly attached.

10

4cm (1.6in)

0.5cm (0.2in)

Place a sheet of raspberry dough (frozen), measuring 4cm (1.6in) wide and 0.5cm (0.2in) thick on top of step 9, which has been turned upside down.

Turn step 10 the right side up again and ensure that all the parts stick to each other.
⇒Freeze for 30 mins or more.

Bake for 15 mins in an oven preheated to 170°C/338°F, then lower the temperature to 160°C/320°F and finish by baking for another 5–8 mins.

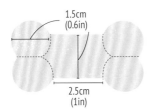

1.5cm (0.6in)

2.5cm (1in)

BONE

Use leftover dough to make some bone cookies. You can decide the size depending on how much leftover dough you have. If you offer the bone cookies as a set together with the dog cookies, it will all match up very well.

INGREDIENTS

(Finished cookie is about 120g / 4.23oz)
*For making dough from scratch

Unsalted butter........... 30g / 1.06oz	1 pinch of salt
Powdered sugar .... 23g / 0.81oz	Cake flour .... 25g / 0.88oz
Whole egg...................... 8g / 0.28oz	Almond flour .... 5g / 0.18oz

METHOD

1 Attach four cylindrical pieces of plain dough (room temperature), with a diameter of 1.5cm (0.6in) to a square-side piece of plain dough (room temperature), measuring 2.5cm (1in) wide and 1.5cm (0.6in) high.
2 Ensure the parts stick together well in the shape of a bone.
⇒Freeze for 30 mins
3 Cut into 0.7–0.8cm (0.3in) thick slices and bake for 15 mins in an oven preheated to 170°C/338°F, then lower the temperature to 160°C/320°F and finish by baking for another 3 mins.

*Any leftover dough can be made into sheets for making cut-out cookies.

BIRD
(COCKATIEL)

MAKE THE BASIC PARTS

*All parts are 8cm (3.1in) in length.

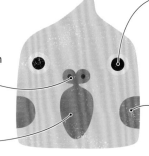

STEPE
A cylindrical piece of strawberry dough (frozen) with a diameter of 0.5cm (0.2in).

BEAK
A bullet-shaped piece of strawberry dough (frozen) 1.5cm (0.6in) wide and 2.5cm (1in) high.

EYE
Make an eye by wrapping a sheet of plain dough (room temperature) 3cm (1.2in) wide and 0.2cm (0.1in) thick, around a cylinder of black cocoa dough (frozen) with a diameter of 0.5cm (0.2in). Make two of these parts.

CHEEK
Cut a cylinder of raspberry dough (frozen) with a 1.5cm (0.6in) diameter in half to make two semi-circular parts.

METHOD

1 Use the ★ ingredients to make the butter dough. (See p. 64.)
2 Add the ♥ ingredients to make up the five different colored doughs.

- ●Red: Raspberry (about 25g / 0.88oz)
  - ★Butter dough ....13g / 0.46oz
  - ♥Cake flour ....9g / 0.32oz
  -   Almond flour.......................2g / 0.07oz
  -   Raspberry powder ....2g / 0.07oz

- ●Black: Black cocoa (about 20g / 0.71oz)
  - ★Butter dough ....10g / 0.35oz
  - ♥Cake flour ....7g / 0.25oz
  -   Almond flour.......................2g / 0.07oz
  -   Black cocoa powder...........2g / 0.07oz

- ●White: Plain (about 20g / 0.71oz)
  - ★Butter dough ....10g / 0.35oz
  - ♥Cake flour ....8g / 0.28oz
  -   Almond flour.......................2g / 0.07oz

1

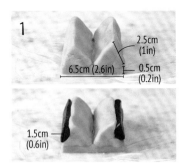

Place two triangular pieces of pumpkin dough (room temperature) on a sheet of pumpkin dough (frozen). Attach the semi-cylindrical pieces of raspberry dough (frozen). Ensure that the raspberry dough pieces are pushed into the pumpkin dough.

2

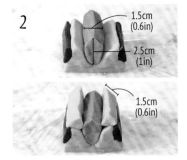

Place the bullet-shaped piece of strawberry dough (frozen) in the middle of step 1 and attach two triangular pieces of pumpkin dough (room temperature) on either side of the strawberry dough, ensuring they stick together well.

3

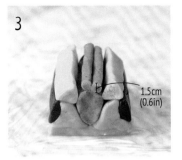

Place two cylindrical pieces of strawberry dough (room temperature) with a diameter of 1.5cm (0.6in), on top of step 2.

4

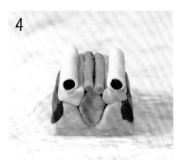

Place the parts for the eyes (see p. 74) on top of step 3.
⇒Freeze for 15–20 mins.

5

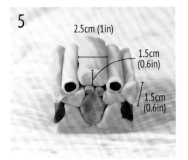

Place two triangular pieces of pumpkin dough (room temperature) on either side of the eyes. Then place a square-shaped piece of pumpkin dough (room temperature) above the nose and between the eyes.
⇒Freeze for 15–20 mins.

FINISHED COCKATIEL

Place a triangular piece of pumpkin dough (room temperature) on top of step 5. Finish off by ensuring that the shape of the head is just right.
⇒Freeze for 30 mins or longer.

Cut into 0.7–0.8cm (0.3in) thick slices and bake for 15 mins in an oven preheated to 170°C/338°F, then lower the temperature to 160°C/320°F and finish by baking for another 5 mins.

★Butter dough (about 185g / 6.53oz)
Unsalted butter...............93g / 3.28oz
Powdered sugar ....70g / 2.47oz
Whole egg........................24g / 0.85oz
2 pinches of salt

●Black: Black cocoa
 (about 230g / 8.11oz)
★Butter dough ....115g / 4.06oz
♥Cake flour ....80g / 2.82oz
 Almond flour....................16g / 0.56oz
 Black cocoa powder.........12g / 0.42oz
 Cocoa powder ....7g / 0.25oz

○White: Plain (about 60g / 2.12oz)
★Butter dough ....30g / 1.06oz
♥Cake flour ....25g / 0.88oz
 Almond flour.......................5g / 0.18oz

*Depending on the person who makes it, the size
of the parts may vary so the amounts for the
ingredients are on the generous side.

BIRD
(JAVA SPARROW)

MAKE THE BASIC PARTS

*All parts are 8cm (3.1in) in length.

EYE
Make an eye by wrapping a
sheet of strawberry dough
(room temperature) 3cm (1.2in)
wide and 0.2cm (0.1in) thick,
around a cylinder of black
cocoa dough (frozen) with a
diameter of 0.5cm (0.2in). Make
two of these parts.

BEAK
A fan-shaped piece of
strawberry dough (frozen)
measuring 2.5cm (1in) wide
and 2cm (0.8in) high.

- ●Pink: Strawberry (about 55g / 1.94oz)
- ★Butter dough ....27g / 0.95oz
- ♥Cake flour ....19g / 0.67oz
-    Almond flour.......................4g / 0.14oz
-    Strawberry powder............5g / 0.18oz

- ●Red: Raspberry (about 20g / 0.71oz)
- ★Butter dough ....10g / 0.35oz
- ♥Cake flour ....7g / 0.25oz
-    Almond flour.......................2g / 0.07oz
-    Raspberry powder ....2g / 0.07oz

METHOD

1. Use the ★ ingredients to make the butter dough. (See p. 64.)
2. Add the ♥ ingredients to make up the four different colored doughs.

1

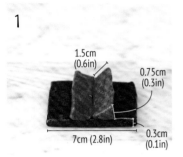

Cut a triangular piece of raspberry dough (room temperature) into half of the thickness. Place these two pieces of the raspberry dough, on top of a sheet of black cocoa dough (frozen) measuring 7cm (2.8in) wide and 0.3cm (0.1in) thick.

2

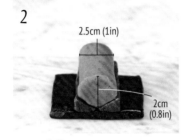

Place the fan-shaped piece of strawberry dough (frozen) measuring 2.5cm (1in) wide and 2cm (0.8in) high, on top of step 1. ⇒Freeze for 15 mins.

3

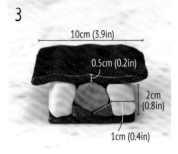

Place two pieces of plain dough (room temperature) on either side of step 2. Then cover this with a sheet of black cocoa dough (room temperature) measuring 10cm (3.9in) wide and 0.5cm (0.2in) thick.

4

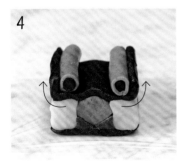

Make two parts for the eyes (see p. 74) and place these on top of step 3. Roll the sheet of black cocoa dough up around the sides of the eyes. Ensure that the parts all stick together.

5

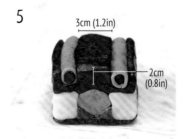

Place a square-shaped piece of black cocoa dough (room temperature) on the top of step 4 between the eyes. Fill in any gaps. ⇒Freeze for 15 mins.

FINISHED JAVA SPARROW

Place a sheet of black cocoa dough (room temperature) on the top of step 5. The Java Sparrow is finished after ensuring that all the parts stick together.
⇒Freeze for 30 mins or longer.

Cut into 0.7–0.8cm (0.3in) thick slices and bake for 15 mins in an oven preheated to 170°C/338°F, then lower the temperature to 160°C/320°F and finish by baking for another 5 mins.

★Butter dough (about 220g / 7.76oz)
Unsalted butter.............110g / 3.88oz
Powdered sugar................83g / 2.93oz
Whole egg.........................30g / 1.06oz
2 pinches of salt

●Purple: Purple sweet potato
(about 330g / 11.6oz)
★Butter dough ....165g / 5.82oz
♥Cake flour ....119g / 4.2oz
Purple sweet potato powder
....23g / 0.81oz
Almond flour.....................23g / 0.81oz

●Yellow: Pumpkin (about 35g / 1.23oz)
★Butter dough ....18g / 0.63oz
♥Cake flour ....13g / 0.46oz
Almond flour.......................2g / 0.07oz
Pumpkin powder...............3g / 0.11oz

*Depending on the person who makes it, the size
of the parts may vary so the amounts for the
ingredients are on the generous side.

BIRD
(BUDGERIGAR)

*All parts are 8cm (3.1in) in length.

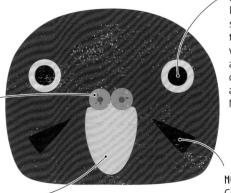

EYE
Make an eye by wrapping a
sheet of plain dough (room
temperature) 3cm (1.2in)
wide and 0.2cm (0.1in) thick,
around a cylinder of black
cocoa dough (frozen) with
a diameter of 0.5cm (0.2in).
Make two of these parts.

STEPE
Two cylindrical pieces of
sesame dough (frozen)
measuring 0.5cm (0.2in)
in diameter.

MOTIF
Cut a triangular piece of
black cocoa dough (frozen)
measuring 1.5cm (0.6in) on
each side, so that one side
measures 0.75cm (0.3in).

BEAK
A bullet-shaped piece of
pumpkin dough (frozen)
measuring 1.8cm (0.7in) on the
base and 2cm (0.8in) high.

- ●Black: Black cocoa (about 25g / 0.88oz)
- ★Butter dough ....13g / 0.46oz
- ♥Cake flour ....9g / 0.32oz
  Almond flour........................ 2g / 0.07oz
  Black cocoa powder........... 2g / 0.07oz

- ●White: Plain (about 20g / 0.71oz)
- ★Butter dough .... 10g / 0.35oz
- ♥Cake flour ....8g / 0.28oz
  Almond flour...................2g / 0.07oz

- ●Gray: Black sesame (about 20g / 0.71oz)
- ★Butter dough ....10g / 0.35oz
- ♥Cake flour ....7g / 0.25oz
  Almond flour........................ 2g / 0.07oz
  Ground sesame (black)..... 2g / 0.07oz
  Black sesame paste ....a small amount

METHOD

1 Use the ★ ingredients to make the butter dough. (See p. 64.)
2 Add the ♥ ingredients to make up the five different colored doughs.

1	2	3

7cm (2.8in)

Make a sheet of purple sweet potato dough (frozen) measuring 7cm (2.8in) wide and 0.3cm (0.1in) thick.

2.5cm (1in)

Place two triangular pieces of purple sweet potato dough (room temperature) measuring 2.5cm (1in) on one side, on top of step 1.

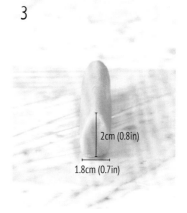

2cm (0.8in)

1.8cm (0.7in)

Make a bullet-shaped piece of pumpkin dough (frozen) measuring 1.8cm (0.7in) on the base and 2cm (0.8in) high.
⇒Freeze for 15–20 mins.

4

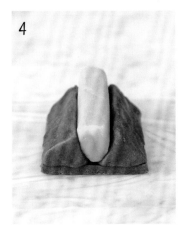

Turn step 3 upside down and insert it in between the two triangular pieces of dough of step 2. Ensure the parts stick together.
⇒Freeze for 15–20 mins.

5

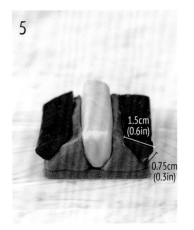

1.5cm (0.6in)

0.75cm (0.3in)

Cut in half a triangular piece of black cocoa dough (frozen) measuring 1.5cm (0.6in) on each side so that one side measures 0.75cm (0.3in). Place these two pieces on the sides of step 4. Ensure the pieces stick together.
⇒Freeze for 15–20 mins.

6

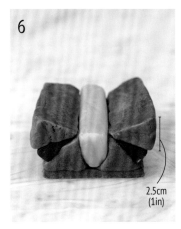

2.5cm (1in)

Place two pieces of purple sweet potato dough (room temperature) measuring 2.5cm (1in) on each side on top of step 5.

7

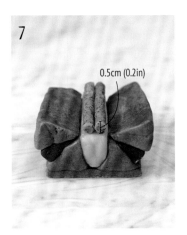

0.5cm (0.2in)

Place two cylindrical pieces of sesame dough (frozen) measuring 0.5cm (0.2in) in diameter on top of step 6.

8

5cm (2in)

0.5cm (0.2in)

Place a sheet of purple sweet potato dough (room temperature) measuring 5cm (2in) wide and 0.5cm (0.2in) thick, on top of step 7.

9

Make two parts for the eyes (see p. 74) and place these on top of step 8.

10

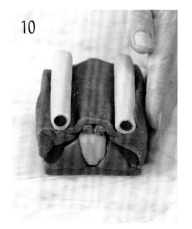

Push the purple sweet potato dough up along the sides of the eye parts and ensure it all sticks together.
⇒Freeze for 15–20 mins.

11

3.5cm (1.4in)

1.5cm (0.6in)

Place a sheet of purple sweet potato dough (room temperature) measuring 3.5cm (1.4in) wide and 1.5cm (0.6in) thick, on top of step 10 and ensure it all sticks together.

12

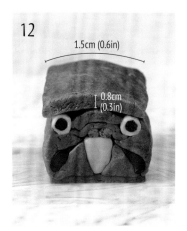

1.5cm (0.6in)

0.8cm (0.3in)

Place a sheet of purple sweet potato dough (room temperature) measuring 9cm (3.5in) wide and 0.8cm (0.3in) thick, on top of step 11.

FINISHED BUDGERIGAR

The Budgerigar is finished after ensuring that all the parts in step 12 stick together.
⇒Freeze for 30 mins or longer.

Cut into 0.7–0.8cm (0.3in) thick slices and bake for 15 mins in an oven preheated to 170°C/338°F, then lower the temperature to 160°C/320°F and finish by baking for another 5 mins.

★Butter dough (about 175g / 6.17oz)
Unsalted butter..................88g / 3.1oz
Powdered sugar ....66g / 2.33oz
Whole egg.........................23g / 0.81oz
2 pinches of salt

●Red: Raspberry (about 90g / 3.17oz)
★Butter dough ....45g / 1.59oz
♥Cake flour ....34g / 1.2oz
Almond flour........................6g / 0.21oz
Raspberry powder ....5g / 0.18oz

●Yellow: Pumpkin (about 80g / 2.82oz)
★Butter dough ....40g / 1.41oz
♥Cake flour ....29g / 1.02oz
Almond flour........................6g / 0.21oz
Pumpkin powder...............6g / 0.21oz

*Depending on the person who makes it, the size of the parts may vary so the amounts for the ingredients are on the generous side.

07

RAINBOW

METHOD

1 Use the ★ ingredients to make the butter dough. (See p. 64.)
2 Add the ♥ ingredients to make up the five different colored doughs.

MAKE THE BASIC PARTS

*All parts are 8cm (3.1in) in length.

5TH LAYER
Sheet of raspberry dough (room temperature) 16cm (6.3in) wide and 0.5cm (0.2in) thick.

4TH LAYER
Sheet of pumpkin dough (room temperature) 14cm (5.5in) wide and 0.5cm (0.2in) thick.

2ND LAYER
Sheet of matcha dough (room temperature) 10cm (3.9in) wide and 0.5cm (0.2in) thick.

3RD LAYER
Sheet of plain dough (room temperature) 12cm (4.7in) wide and 0.5cm (0.2in) thick.

1ST LAYER
Sheet of purple sweet potato dough (room temperature) 8cm (3.1in) wide and 0.5cm (0.2in) thick.

White: Plain (about 70g / 2.47oz)
★Butter dough .... 35g / 1.23oz
♥Cake flour .... 29g / 1.02oz
Almond flour .... 6g / 0.21oz

Green: Matcha (about 55g / 1.94oz)
★Butter dough .... 28g / 1oz
♥Cake flour .... 20g / 0.71oz
Almond flour .... 4g / 0.14oz
Matcha powder .... 3g / 0.11oz

Purple: Purple sweet potato (about 45g / 1.59oz)
★Butter dough .... 23g / 0.81oz
♥Cake flour .... 16g / 0.56oz
Almond flour .... 3g / 0.11oz
Purple sweet potato powder
.... 3g / 0.11oz

1

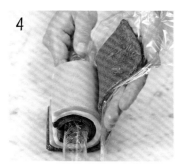

Wrap the first layer around a cylinder with a diameter of 2cm (0.8in).
⇒Freeze for 15 mins.

2

Wrap the second layer around step 1 and ensure that it sticks together.
⇒Freeze for 15 mins.

3

Wrap the third and fourth layers around step 2 and ensure that it all sticks together.
⇒Freeze for 15 mins.

4

Wrap the fifth layer around step 3.

5

Neaten up the final shape and ensure that it all sticks together.

FINISHED RAINBOW

Finish by removing the cylinder and cutting off any surplus.
⇒Freeze for 30 mins or longer.

Cut into 0.7–0.8cm (0.3in) thick slices and bake for 15 mins in an oven preheated to 170°C/338°F, then lower the temperature to 160°C/320°F and finish by baking for another 5–8 mins.

★Butter dough (about 220g / 7.76oz)
Unsalted butter............110g / 3.88oz
Powdered sugar..............82g / 2.89oz
Whole egg........................30g / 1.06oz
2 pinches of salt

●Green: Matcha (about 220g / 7.76oz)
★Butter dough ....110g / 3.88oz
♥Cake flour.........................82g / 2.89oz
Almond flour....................15g / 0.53oz
Matcha powder ....13g / 0.46oz

●Yellow: Pumpkin (about 175g / 6.17oz)
★Butter dough ....88g / 3.1oz
♥Cake flour ....63g / 2.22oz
Almond flour....................12g / 0.42oz
Pumpkin powder.............12g / 0.42oz

*Depending on the person who makes it, the size of the parts may vary so the amounts for the ingredients are on the generous side.

FROG

MAKE THE BASIC PARTS *All parts are 8cm (3.1in) in length.

EYE
Make an eye by wrapping a sheet of pumpkin dough (room temperature) 5cm (2in) wide and 0.2cm (0.1in) thick, around a cylinder of black cocoa dough (frozen) with a diameter of 1cm (0.4in). Make two of these parts.

- ● Black: Black cocoa (about 30g / 1.06oz)
- ★ Butter dough .... 13g / 0.46oz
- ♥ Cake flour .... 13g / 0.46oz
-    Almond flour .... 2g / 0.07oz
-    Black cocoa powder .... 2g / 0.07oz

METHOD

1 Use the ★ ingredients to make the butter dough. (See p. 64.)
2 Add the ♥ ingredients to make up the three different colored doughs.

1

Make two eye parts (see p. 74) and wrap each part in a sheet of matcha dough (room temperature) 6cm (2.4in) wide and 0.2cm (0.1in) thick.
⇒Freeze for 15 mins.

2

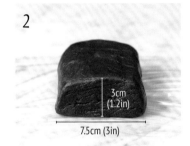

Make a semi-cylindrical piece of matcha dough (room temperature) measuring 7.5cm (3in) at the base and 3cm (1.2in) high.

3

Using a chopstick, make two depressions about 1cm (0.4in) deep on the top of step 2.

4

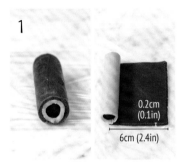

Place the two eye parts from step 1 in the depressions of step 3. Fill in any gaps and ensure everything sticks together.
⇒Freeze for 15–20 mins.

5

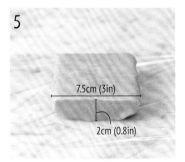

Make a semi-cylindrical piece of pumpkin dough (room temperature) measuring 7.5cm (3in) at the base and 2cm (0.8in) high.

FINISHED FROG

Finish the Frog by placing step 4 on top of step 5 and making sure the two pieces of dough stick together well.
⇒Freeze for 30 mins or longer.

Cut into 0.7–0.8cm (0.3in) thick slices and bake for 15 mins in an oven preheated to 170°C/338°F, then lower the temperature to 160°C/320°F and finish by baking for another 5–8 mins.

INGREDIENTS

★Butter dough (about 260g / 9.17oz)
Unsalted butter.............130g / 4.59oz
Powdered sugar..............99g / 3.49oz
Whole egg...........................34g / 1.2oz
3 pinches of salt

●Purple: Purple sweet potato
(about 360g / 12.7oz)
★Butter dough ....180g / 6.35oz
♥Cake flour.......................130g / 4.59oz
Almond flour.....................25g / 0.88oz
Purple sweet potato powder
.....................................25g / 0.88oz

●Yellow: Pumpkin (about 125g / 4.41oz)
★Butter dough ....63g / 2.22oz
♥Cake flour..........................45g / 1.59oz
Almond flour......................9g / 0.32oz
Pumpkin powder...............9g / 0.32oz

*Depending on the person who makes it, the size
of the parts may vary so the amounts for the
ingredients are on the generous side.

FLOWER

MAKE THE BASIC PARTS   *All parts are 8cm (3.1in) in length.

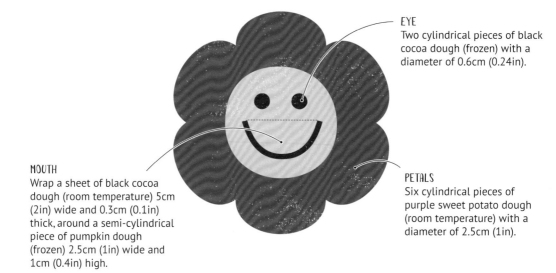

EYE
Two cylindrical pieces of black cocoa dough (frozen) with a diameter of 0.6cm (0.24in).

MOUTH
Wrap a sheet of black cocoa dough (room temperature) 5cm (2in) wide and 0.3cm (0.1in) thick, around a semi-cylindrical piece of pumpkin dough (frozen) 2.5cm (1in) wide and 1cm (0.4in) high.

PETALS
Six cylindrical pieces of purple sweet potato dough (room temperature) with a diameter of 2.5cm (1in).

● Black: Black cocoa (about 30g / 1.06oz)
★ Butter dough .... 15g / 0.53oz
♥ Cake flour .... 10g / 0.35oz
   Almond flour........................ 2g / 0.07oz
   Black cocoa powder........... 3g / 0.11oz

METHOD

1 Use the ★ ingredients to make the butter dough. (See p. 64.)
2 Add the ♥ ingredients to make up the three different colored doughs.

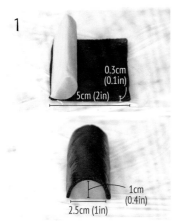

1

0.3cm (0.1in)
5cm (2in)

1cm (0.4in)
2.5cm (1in)

Wrap a sheet of black cocoa dough (room temperature) 5cm (2in) wide and 0.3cm (0.1in) thick, around the curved part of a semi-cylindrical piece of pumpkin dough (frozen) measuring 2.5cm (1in) wide and 1cm (0.4in) high.
⇒Freeze for 15 mins.

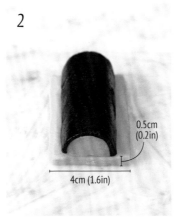

2

0.5cm (0.2in)
4cm (1.6in)

Place step 1 on top of a sheet of pumpkin dough (room temperature) measuring 4cm (1.6in) wide and 0.5cm (0.2in) thick.

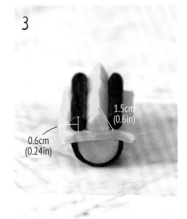

3

1.5cm (0.6in)
0.6cm (0.24in)

Turn step 2 upside down and place a triangular piece of pumpkin dough (room temperature) measuring 1.5cm (0.6in) on each side, in between two cylindrical pieces of black cocoa dough (frozen) with a diameter of 0.6cm (0.24in).

4

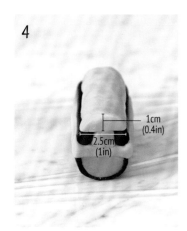

Make a semi-cylindrical piece of pumpkin dough (room temperature) measuring 2.5cm (1in) wide and 1cm (0.4in) high. Place it on top of step 3 and ensure that the shape is nice and round.
⇒Freeze for 15 mins.

5

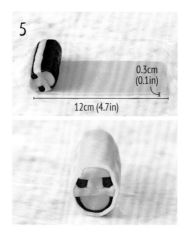

Wrap step 4in a sheet of pumpkin dough (room temperature) 12cm (4.7in) wide and 0.3cm (0.1in) thick.
⇒Freeze for 15 mins.

6

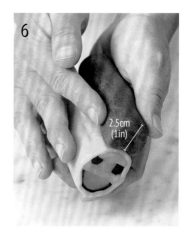

Make six cylindrical pieces of purple sweet potato dough (room temperature) with a diameter of 2.5cm (1in). Attach the pieces one by one to step 5, ensuring that each piece sticks on properly to the flower's center.

FINISHED FLOWER

Finish by arranging it into the proper shape of a flower.
⇒Freeze for 30 mins or longer.

Cut into 0.7–0.8cm (0.3in) thick slices and bake for 15 mins in an oven preheated to 170°C/338°F, then lower the temperature to 160°C/320°F and finish by baking for another 5–8 mins.

★Butter dough (about 60g / 2.12oz)
  Unsalted butter ....30g / 1.06oz
  Powdered sugar ....23g / 0.81oz
  Whole egg...........................8g / 0.28oz
  1 pinch of salt

●Green: Matcha (about 100g / 3.53oz)
★Butter dough ....50g / 1.76oz
♥Cake flour ....37g / 1.31oz
  Almond flour........................ 7g / 0.25oz
  Matcha powder ....6g / 0.21oz

●White: Plain (about 20g / 0.71oz)
★Butter dough ....10g / 0.35oz
♥Cake flour ....8g / 0.28oz
  Almond flour......................2g / 0.07oz

*Depending on the person who makes it, the size of the parts may vary so the amounts for the ingredients are on the generous side.

09 LEAF

*All parts are 8cm (3.1in) in length.

VEIN OF THE LEAF
A sheet of plain dough (frozen) 5.5cm (2.2in) wide and 0.2cm (0.1in) thick.

METHOD

1 Use the ★ ingredients to make the butter dough. (See p. 64.)
2 Add the ♥ ingredients to make up the two different colored doughs.

1

5.5cm (2.2in)
1cm (0.4in)

Make a piece of matcha dough (room temperature) in the shape of a leaf measuring 5.5cm (2.2in) wide and 1cm (0.4in) high. Cut this in half with a knife.

2

5.5cm (2.2in)
0.2cm (0.1in)

Place a sheet of plain dough (frozen) 5.5cm (2.2in) wide and 0.2cm (0.1in) thick between the two pieces of step 1.

FINISHED LEAF

Finish the Leaf by fixing up the shape and ensuring the parts stick together.
⇒Freeze for 30 mins or longer.

Cut into 0.7–0.8cm (0.3in) thick slices and bake for 15 mins in an oven preheated to 170°C/338°F, then lower the temperature to 160°C/320°F and finish by baking for another 3 mins.

★Butter dough (about 260g / 9.17oz)
Unsalted butter............ 130g / 4.59oz
Powdered sugar .... 99g / 3.49oz
Whole egg........................ 34g / 1.2oz
3 pinches of salt

⬤White: Plain (about 290g / 10.2oz)
★Butter dough .... 145g / 5.11oz
♥Cake flour .... 119g / 4.2oz
Almond flour.................... 26g / 0.92oz

*Depending on the person who makes it, the size of the parts may vary so the amounts for the ingredients are on the generous side.

⬤Brown: Cocoa (about 170g / 6oz)
★Butter dough .... 85g / 3oz
♥Cake flour .... 61g / 2.15oz
Almond flour.................... 12g / 0.42oz
Cocoa powder .... 12g / 0.42oz

10
SQUIRREL

MAKE THE BASIC PARTS
*All parts are 8cm (3.1in) in length.

MOUTH
The mouth is made up of a sheet of strawberry dough (room temperature) 3cm (1.2in) wide and 0.2cm (0.1in) thick, and another sheet of strawberry dough (room temperature) 2cm (0.8in) wide and 0.2cm (0.1in) thick, wrapped around two cylinders of plain dough (frozen) with a diameter of 1cm (0.4in). Completing the mouth is the chin which is a triangular piece of plain dough (room temperature) measuring 1.5cm (0.6in) on each side, and fitted into the space under the strawberry doughs.

EAR
Two triangular pieces of cocoa dough (frozen) measuring 1cm (0.4in) on each side.

EYE
Make an eye by wrapping a sheet of plain dough (room temperature) 4.5cm (1.8in) wide and 0.2cm (0.1in) thick, around an oval-shaped cylinder of black cocoa dough (frozen) measuring 1.2cm (0.5in) wide and 0.5cm (0.2in) high. Make two of these parts.

STEPE
A triangular piece of strawberry dough (frozen) measuring 1cm (0.4in) on each side.

● Pink: Strawberry (about 30g / 1.06oz)
★ Butter dough ....15g / 0.53oz
♥ Cake flour ....10g / 0.35oz
   Almond flour........................ 2g / 0.07oz
   Strawberry powder............3g / 0.11oz

● Black: Black cocoa (about 20g / 0.71oz)
★ Butter dough ....10g / 0.35oz
♥ Cake flour .... 7g / 0.25oz
   Almond flour........................ 2g / 0.07oz
   Black cocoa powder........... 2g / 0.07oz

METHOD

1 Use the ★ ingredients to make the butter dough. (See p. 64.)
2 Add the ♥ ingredients to make up the four different colored doughs.

1

Make the nose and the mouth parts. (See p. 74.)
⇒Freeze for 15 mins.

2

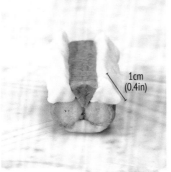

1cm (0.4in)

Fit two triangular pieces of plain dough (room temperature), measuring 1cm (0.4in) on each side, on the left and right sides of the nose. Gently push the parts together to fill in any gaps and make them stick to each other.

3

1.5cm (0.6in)

8–9cm (3.1–3.5in)

Make a sheet using 200g (7.05oz) of plain dough (room temperature) 8–9cm (3.1–3.5in) wide and 1.5cm (0.6in) thick. Place step 2 on top of this sheet.

4

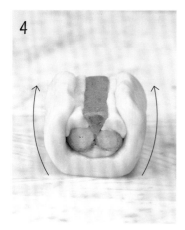

Use the sheet to wrap the parts of step 2 up to the sides and ensure it all sticks together.

5

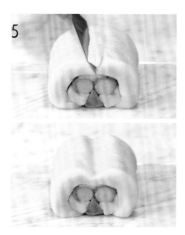

Turn step 4 upside down and use a knife to cut the center, taking out a small piece. Smooth over the cut edges.
⇒Freeze for 15–20 mins.

6

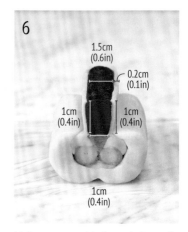

1.5cm (0.6in)

0.2cm (0.1in)

1cm (0.4in)

1cm (0.4in)

1cm (0.4in)

Make a trapezoid-shaped piece of cocoa dough (frozen) and sandwich this between two sheets of plain dough (room temperature). Place all of this on top of step 5 and ensure it all sticks together.
⇒Freeze for 5 mins.

7

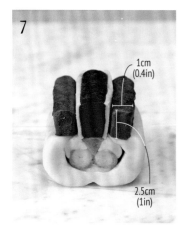

1cm (0.4in)

2.5cm (1in)

Make two square-shaped pieces of cocoa dough (room temperature) measuring 1cm (0.4in) wide and 2.5cm (1in) thick. Place these on either side of the middle of step 6 and ensure it all sticks together, while pushing it all towards the center.

8

Make two parts for the eyes (see p. 74) and place them on top of step 7.
⇒Freeze for 15–20 mins.

9

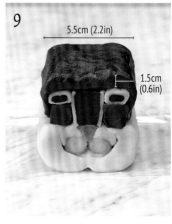

5.5cm (2.2in)

1.5cm (0.6in)

Place a thin semi-cylindrical piece of cocoa dough (room temperature) measuring 5.5cm (2.2in) wide and 1.5cm (0.6in) thick, on top of step 8. Fill in the gaps and ensure it all sticks together.
⇒Freeze for 15–20 mins.

1cm
(0.4in)

The Squirrel is finished after placing two triangular pieces of cocoa dough (frozen) measuring 1cm (0.4in) on each side, on top of step 9 and ensuring it all sticks together.
⇒Freeze for 30 mins or longer.

Cut into 0.7–0.8cm (0.3in) thick slices and bake for 15 mins in an oven preheated to 170°C/338°F, then lower the temperature to 160°C/320°F and finish by baking for another 5–8 mins.

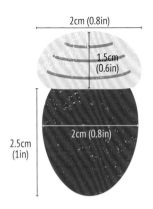

2cm (0.8in)

1.5cm
(0.6in)

2.5cm
(1in)

2cm (0.8in)

ACORN

Let's make acorn-shaped cookies using the leftover dough. This is an easy motif that combines two parts.

INGREDIENTS

*If making new dough.
★Butter dough (about 38g / 1.34oz)
  Unsalted butter ....19g / 0.67oz
  Powdered sugar ...... 15g / 0.53oz
  Whole egg ....5g / 0.18oz
  1 pinch of salt
■ Beige: Kinako (about 25g / 0.88oz)
★Butter dough .... 13g / 0.46oz
♥Cake flour ....9g / 0.32oz
  Almond flour ....2g / 0.07oz
  Kinako ....2g / 0.07oz
● Brown: Cocoa (about 50g / 1.76oz)
★Butter dough .... 25g / 0.88oz
♥Cake flour ....18g / 0.63oz
  Almond flour ....4g / 0.14oz
  Cocoa powder..........4g / 0.14oz

METHOD

1 Make a bullet-shaped piece of cocoa dough (frozen) measuring 2cm (0.8in) wide and 2.5cm (1in) high. Combine this with a semi-cylindrical piece of kinako dough (room temperature) measuring 2cm (0.8in) wide and 1.5cm (0.6in) high.

2 Ensure that the two parts stick to each other and finish off the shape into that of an acorn. ⇒Freeze for 5 mins.

3 Cut into 0.7–0.8cm (0.3in) thick slices and use a toothpick to draw lines on the cap of the acorn.

4 Bake for 15 mins in an oven preheated to 170°C/338°F.
  *Any leftover dough can be made into sheets for making cut-out cookies.

★Butter dough (about 300g / 10.6oz)
Unsalted butter............150g / 5.29oz
Powdered sugar ....112g / 3.95oz
Whole egg.......................40g / 1.41oz
3 pinches of salt

● Beige: Kinako (about 300g / 10.6oz)
★Butter dough ....150g / 5.29oz
♥Cake flour ....108g / 3.81oz
Almond flour....................21g / 0.74oz
Kinako..............................21g / 0.74oz

● White: Plain (about 230g / 8.11oz)
★Butter dough ....115g / 4.06oz
♥Cake flour ....94g / 3.32oz
Almond flour....................21g / 0.74oz

*Depending on the person who makes it, the size
 of the parts may vary so the amounts for the
 ingredients are on the generous side.

11

SHEEP

MAKE THE BASIC PARTS   *All parts are 8cm (3.1in) in length.

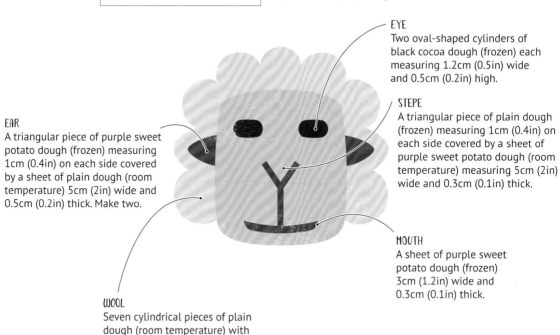

EYE
Two oval-shaped cylinders of
black cocoa dough (frozen) each
measuring 1.2cm (0.5in) wide
and 0.5cm (0.2in) high.

STEPE
A triangular piece of plain dough
(frozen) measuring 1cm (0.4in) on
each side covered by a sheet of
purple sweet potato dough (room
temperature) measuring 5cm (2in)
wide and 0.3cm (0.1in) thick.

EAR
A triangular piece of purple sweet
potato dough (frozen) measuring
1cm (0.4in) on each side covered
by a sheet of plain dough (room
temperature) 5cm (2in) wide and
0.5cm (0.2in) thick. Make two.

MOUTH
A sheet of purple sweet
potato dough (frozen)
3cm (1.2in) wide and
0.3cm (0.1in) thick.

WOOL
Seven cylindrical pieces of plain
dough (room temperature) with
a diameter of 1.5cm (0.6in).

- Purple: Purple sweet potato
  (about 45g / 1.59oz)
  - ★ Butter dough .... 23g / 0.81oz
  - ♥ Cake flour .... 16g / 0.56oz
  - Almond flour .... 3g / 0.11oz
  - Purple sweet potato powder
    .... 3g / 0.11oz

- Black: Black cocoa (about 20g / 0.71oz)
  - ★ Butter dough .... 10g / 0.35oz
  - ♥ Cake flour .... 7g / 0.25oz
  - Almond flour .... 2g / 0.07oz
  - Black cocoa powder .... 2g / 0.07oz

METHOD

1 Use the ★ ingredients to make the
  butter dough. (See p. 64.)

2 Add the ♥ ingredients to make up
  the four different colored doughs.

1

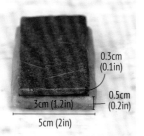

Place a sheet of purple sweet
potato dough (frozen) measuring
3cm (1.2in) wide and 0.3cm (0.1in)
thick, on top of a sheet of kinako
dough (frozen) measuring 5cm
(2in) wide and 0.5cm (0.2in) thick.

2

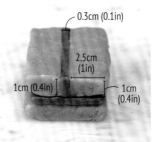

Sandwich a bar of purple sweet
potato dough (frozen) measuring
1cm (0.4in) wide and 0.3cm (0.1in)
thick, between two sheets of
kinako dough (room temperature)
measuring 2.5cm (1in) wide and
1cm (0.4in) thick.
⇒Freeze for 15 mins.

3

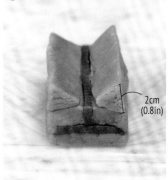

Place two triangular pieces of
kinako dough (room temperature)
measuring 2cm (0.8in) on each
side on top of step 2 and ensure it
all sticks together.

4

Make the part for the nose.
(See p. 72.)
⇒Freeze for 15 mins.

5

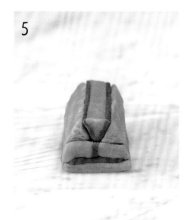

Turn step 4 upside down and place it on top of step 3. Ensure everything sticks together.
⇒Freeze for 15–20 mins.

6

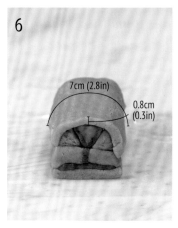

7cm (2.8in)
0.8cm (0.3in)

Place a sheet of kinako dough (room temperature) measuring 7cm (2.8in) wide and 0.8cm (0.3in) thick on top of step 5 and ensure that everything sticks together.

7

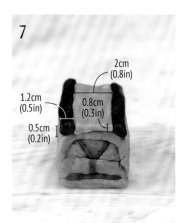

2cm (0.8in)
1.2cm (0.5in)
0.8cm (0.3in)
0.5cm (0.2in)

Place two cylinders of black cocoa dough (frozen) measuring 1.2cm (0.5in) wide and 0.5cm (0.2in) high on top of step 6, together with a sheet of kinako dough (room temperature) 2cm (0.8in) wide and 0.8cm (0.3in) thick. Ensure everything sticks together.

8

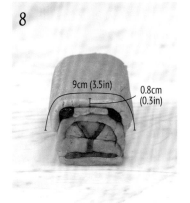

9cm (3.5in)
0.8cm (0.3in)

Place a sheet of kinako dough (room temperature) measuring 9cm (3.5in) wide and 0.8cm (0.3in) thick on top of step 7. Ensure everything sticks together.
⇒Freeze for 15–20 mins.

9

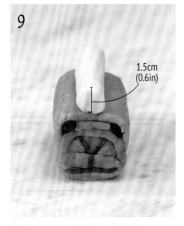

1.5cm (0.6in)

Make seven cylinders of plain dough (room temperature) with a diameter of 1.5cm (0.6in). Place one of the cylinders on top of step 8, in the center. Ensure it is firmly attached.

10

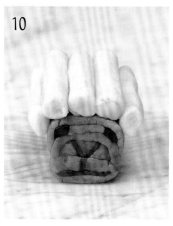

Attach another four cylinders of plain dough to step 9. Make sure they are firmly attached as they come off very easily.

11

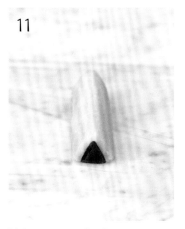

Make two parts for the ears. (See p. 73.)
⇒Freeze for 5 mins.

12

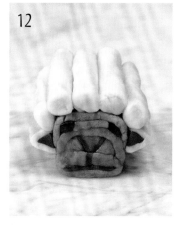

Attach the ear parts to step 10. Make sure they are firmly attached.

FINISHED SHEEP

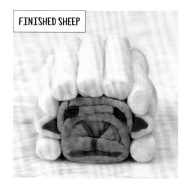

Attach the two remaining cylinders of plain dough to step 12. The Sheep is finished after they have been firmly attached.
⇒Freeze for 30 mins or longer.

Cut into 0.7–0.8cm (0.3in) thick slices and bake for 15 mins in an oven preheated to 170°C/338°F, then lower the temperature to 160°C/320°F and finish by baking for another 5–8 mins.

★Butter dough (about 225g / 7.94oz)
Unsalted butter.............112g / 3.95oz
Powdered sugar.....................85g / 3oz
Whole egg.........................30g / 1.06oz
2 pinches of salt

○White: Plain (about 250g / 8.82oz)
★Butter dough ....125g / 4.41oz
♥Cake flour ....103g / 3.63oz
  Almond flour....................23g / 0.81oz

*Depending on the person who makes it, the size
of the parts may vary so the amounts for the
ingredients are on the generous side.

●Black: Black cocoa
  (about 195g / 6.88oz)
★Butter dough ....100g / 3.53oz
♥Cake flour ....70g / 2.47oz
  Almond flour....................15g / 0.53oz
  Black cocoa powder.........10g / 0.35oz
  Cocoa powder ....5g / 0.18oz

12

PANDA

MAKE THE BASIC PARTS   *All parts are 8cm (3.1in) in length.

EAR
Two semi-cylindrical
pieces of black cocoa
dough (frozen) measuring
2cm (0.8in) wide and
1.5cm (0.6in) high.

MOUTH
A sheet of black cocoa
dough (frozen) 5cm
(2in) wide and 0.3cm
(0.1in) thick.

EYE
Two bullet-shaped pieces of black
cocoa dough (frozen) measuring
1.5cm (0.6in) wide and 2cm
(0.8in) high.

1 Use the ★ ingredients to make the butter dough. (See p. 64.)
2 Add the ♥ ingredients to make up the two different colored doughs.

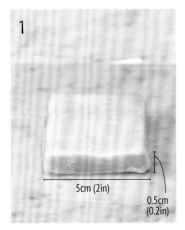

Make a sheet of plain dough (frozen) 5cm (2in) wide and 0.5cm (0.2in) thick.

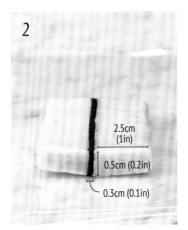

Cut the sheet of plain dough (room temperature) in step 1 into two pieces measuring 2.5cm (1in) wide and 0.5cm (0.2in) thick. Sandwich a sheet of black cocoa dough (frozen) 0.5cm (0.2in) wide and 0.3cm (0.1in) thick, between the two pieces of plain dough.
⇒Freeze for 5 mins.

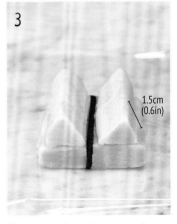

Place two triangular pieces of plain dough (room temperature) measuring 1.5cm (0.6in) on each side on top of step 2.

4

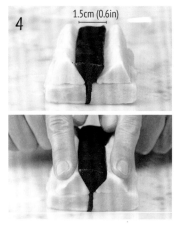

1.5cm (0.6in)

Place a triangular piece of black cocoa dough (room temperature) measuring 1.5cm (0.6in) on each side, on top of step 3. Push with your fingers to fill in any gaps and ensure that it all sticks together.
⇒Freeze for 15 mins.

5

2.5cm (1in)

Place a triangular piece of plain dough (room temperature) measuring 2.5cm (1in) on one side on top of step 4.

6

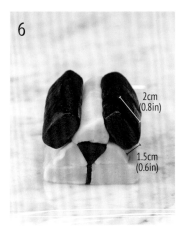

2cm (0.8in)

1.5cm (0.6in)

Place two bullet-shaped pieces of black cocoa dough (frozen) measuring 1.5cm (0.6in) wide and 2cm (0.8in) high on top of step 5.

7

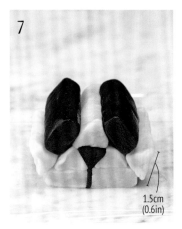

1.5cm (0.6in)

Attach two triangular pieces of plain dough (room temperature) measuring 1.5cm (0.6in) on each side, on either side of step 6.

8

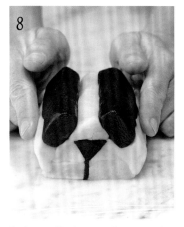

Push step 7 with your fingers to fill in any gaps and ensure that it all sticks together.
⇒Freeze for 15–20 mins.

9

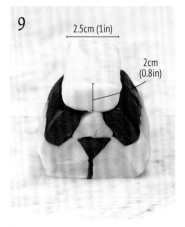

2.5cm (1in)

2cm (0.8in)

Place a square-shaped piece of plain dough (room temperature) measuring 2.5cm (1in) wide and 2cm (0.8in) thick, on top of step 8.

10

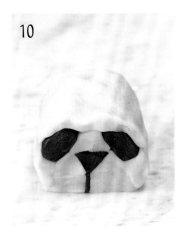

Push step 9 with your fingers so that the piece of plain dough spreads out and covers the eyes.
⇒Freeze for 15–20 mins.

11

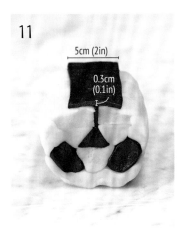

5cm (2in)

0.3cm (0.1in)

Place a sheet of black cocoa dough (frozen) measuring 5cm (2in) wide and 0.3cm (0.1in) thick on top of step 10 turned upside down.

12

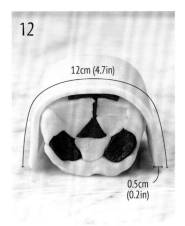

12cm (4.7in)

0.5cm (0.2in)

Cover step 11 with a sheet of plain dough (room temperature) measuring 12cm (4.7in) wide and 0.5cm (0.2in) thick. Ensure that everything sticks together and fix up the shape.

FINISHED PANDA

1.5cm (0.6in)

2cm (0.8in)

Turn step 12 the right way up again and attach two semi-cylindrical pieces of black cocoa dough (frozen). The Panda is finished after ensuring that all the parts stick together well.
⇒Freeze for 30 mins or longer.

Cut into 0.7–0.8cm (0.3in) thick slices and bake for 15 mins in an oven preheated to 170°C/338°F, then lower the temperature to 160°C/320°F and finish by baking for another 5–8 mins.

INGREDIENTS

★Butter dough (about 320g / 11.3oz)
Unsalted butter.............160g / 5.64oz
Powdered sugar...........120g / 4.23oz
Whole egg........................43g / 1.52oz
3 pinches of salt

●Brown: Cocoa (about 390g / 13.8oz)
★Butter dough ....195g / 6.88oz
♥Cake flour ....141g / 4.97oz
Almond flour.....................27g / 0.95oz
Cocoa powder ....27g / 0.95oz

●Beige: Kinako (about 160g / 5.64oz)
★Butter dough ....80g / 2.82oz
♥Cake flour ....58g / 2.05oz
Kinako.................................11g / 0.39oz
Almond flour.....................11g / 0.39oz

* Depending on the person who makes it, the size of the parts may vary so the amounts for the ingredients are on the generous side.

13

BEAR

MAKE THE BASIC PARTS   *All parts are 8cm (3.1in) in length.

EAR
Two semi-cylindrical pieces of cocoa dough (frozen) measuring 1.5cm (0.6in) wide and 1cm (0.4in) high.

EYE
Make an eye by wrapping a sheet of plain dough (room temperature) measuring 3.5cm (1.4in) wide and 0.3cm (0.1in) thick, around a cylinder of black cocoa dough (frozen) with a diameter of 0.8cm (0.3in). Make two of these parts.

STEPE
An oval-shaped cylinder of black cocoa dough (frozen) measuring 2cm (0.8in) wide and 1.5cm (0.6in) high.

MOUTH
A sheet of black cocoa dough (frozen) 2cm (0.8in) wide and 0.3cm (0.1in) thick.

- ●Black: Black cocoa (about 60g / 2.12oz)
- ★Butter dough ....30g / 1.06oz
- ♥Cake flour ....21g / 0.74oz
  Almond flour.......................4g / 0.14oz
  Black cocoa powder...........3g / 0.11oz
  Cocoa powder ....2g / 0.07oz

- ○White: Plain (about 25g / 0.88oz)
- ★Butter dough ....13g / 0.46oz
- ♥Cake flour ....10g / 0.35oz
  Almond flour....................... 2g / 0.07oz

METHOD

1. Use the ★ ingredients to make the butter dough. (See p. 64.)
2. Add the ♥ ingredients to make up the four different colored doughs.

1

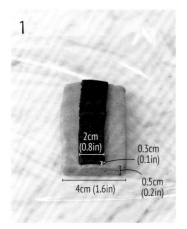

2cm (0.8in)
0.3cm (0.1in)
4cm (1.6in)
0.5cm (0.2in)

Place a sheet of black cocoa dough (frozen) 2cm (0.8in) wide and 0.3cm (0.1in) thick, on top of a sheet of plain dough (frozen) 4cm (1.6in) wide and 0.5cm (0.2in) thick.
⇒Freeze for 5 mins.

2

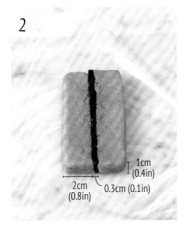

1cm (0.4in)
2cm (0.8in)
0.3cm (0.1in)

Sandwich a piece of black cocoa dough (frozen) measuring 1cm (0.4in) wide and 0.3cm (0.1in) thick, between two sheets of kinako dough (room temperature) 2cm (0.8in) wide and 1cm (0.4in) thick.
⇒Freeze for 5 mins.

3

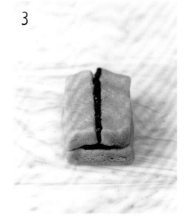

Place step 2 on top of step 1.
⇒Freeze for 5 mins.

4

2cm
(0.8in)

2cm
(0.8in)

1.5cm
(0.6in)

Place two triangular pieces of kinako dough (room temperature on top of step 3. Then place a cylinder of black cocoa dough (frozen) measuring 2cm (0.8in) wide and 1.5cm (0.6in) high, in the center of the two pieces of kinako dough. Fill in any gaps and ensure it all sticks together.

5

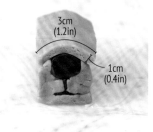

3cm
(1.2in)

1cm
(0.4in)

Place a sheet of kinako dough (room temperature) 3cm (1.2in) wide and 1cm (0.4in) thick on top of step 4. Ensure it all sticks together.
⇒Freeze for 15 mins.

6

1.5cm
(0.6in)

3cm
(1.2in)

10cm (3.9in)

0.5cm
(0.2in)

On a sheet of cocoa dough (room temperature) 10cm (3.9in) wide and 0.5cm (0.2in) thick, place step 5 and two square-shaped pieces of cocoa dough (room temperature) measuring 1.5cm (0.6in) wide and 3cm (1.2in) high. Wrap the sheet up on both sides and ensure it all sticks together.

7

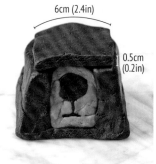

6cm (2.4in)

0.5cm
(0.2in)

Place a sheet of cocoa dough (room temperature) 6cm (2.4in) wide and 0.5cm (0.2in) thick, on top of step 6 and ensure it all sticks together.

8

Make two parts for the eyes (see p. 74) and place them on top of step 7.
⇒Freeze for 15 mins.

9

2cm
(0.8in)

Attach two triangular pieces of cocoa dough (room temperature) measuring 2cm (0.8in) on each side, to the sides of step 8. Fill in any gaps and ensure it sticks together.

10

Place a square-shaped piece of cocoa dough (room temperature) measuring 2.5cm (1in) wide at the base and 2cm (0.8in) high, on top of step 9. Push the dough with your fingers so that it covers the eyes.
⇒Freeze for 15–20 mins.

FINISHED BEAR

Attach two semi-cylindrical pieces of cocoa dough (frozen) measuring 1.5cm (0.6in) on the base and 1cm (0.4in) high, to the top of step 10. The Bear is finished after you lift up the sides to form the bear's cheeks.
⇒Freeze for 30 mins or longer.

Cut into 0.7–0.8cm (0.3in) thick slices and bake for 15 mins in an oven preheated to 170°C/338°F, then lower the temperature to 160°C/320°F and finish by baking for another 5–8 mins.

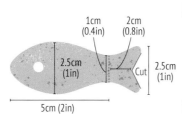

SALMON

Let's try making salmon-shaped cookies. Salmon are the bear's favorite thing to eat. This salmon cookie is bigger than the little fish on p. 79 and looks quite real.

INGREDIENTS

(Finished cookie is about 170g / 6oz)

Unsalted butter............ 43g / 1.52oz	Cake flour.................................... 61g / 2.15oz
Powdered sugar .... 32g / 1.13oz	Ground black sesame............... 12g / 0.42oz
Whole egg..................... 11g / 0.39oz	Almond flour .... 12g / 0.42oz
1 pinch of salt	Black sesame paste....... about ¹/₂ teaspoon

METHOD

1. Combine an oval-shaped piece of black sesame dough (room temperature) measuring 5cm (2in) wide and 2.5cm (1in) high with a trapezoid-shaped piece of ground black sesame dough (room temperature) measuring 2.5cm (1in) on the base and 2cm (0.8in) high.
2. Ensure the pieces stick to each other and fix up the shape.
⇒Freeze for 5 mins.
3. Cut into slices 0.7–0.8cm (0.3in) thick and make a hole for the eye. Cut the tail part with a knife.
4. Bake for 15 mins in an oven preheated to 170°C/338°F, then lower the temperature to 160°C/320°F and finish by baking for another 5–8 mins.

★Butter dough (about 490g / 17.3oz)
Unsalted butter............ 245g / 8.64oz
Powdered sugar .... 184g / 6.49oz
Whole egg........................63g / 2.22oz
5 pinches of salt

●Brown: Cocoa (about 445g / 15.7oz)
★Butter dough .... 223g / 7.87oz
♥Cake flour .... 160g / 5.64oz
Almond flour.....................31g / 1.09oz
Cocoa powder ....31g / 1.09oz

●Yellow: Pumpkin (about 265g / 9.35oz)
★Butter dough .... 133g / 4.69oz
♥Cake flour ....95g / 3.35oz
Almond flour.....................19g / 0.67oz
Pumpkin powder..............19g / 0.67oz

* Depending on the person who makes it, the size of the parts may vary so the amounts for the ingredients are on the generous side.

LION

MAKE THE BASIC PARTS   *All parts are 8cm (3.1in) in length.

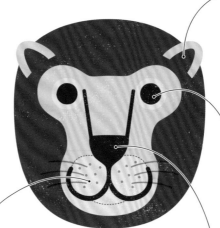

EAR
A triangular piece of cocoa dough (frozen) measuring 1.5cm (0.6in) on each side covered by a sheet of pumpkin dough (room temperature) 5cm (2in) wide and 0.5cm (0.2in) thick. Make two.

EYE
Make an eye by wrapping a sheet of plain dough (room temperature) measuring 5cm (2in) wide and 0.2cm (0.1in) thick, around a cylinder of black cocoa dough (frozen) with a diameter of 1cm (0.4in). Make two of these parts.

MOUTH
The mouth is made up of a sheet of black cocoa dough (room temperature) 6cm (2.4in) wide and 0.3cm (0.1in) thick, and another sheet of black cocoa dough (room temperature) 5cm (2in) wide and 0.3cm (0.1in) thick, wrapped around two cylinders of plain dough (frozen) with a diameter of 2cm (0.8in). Completing the mouth is the chin which is a triangular piece of plain dough (room temperature) measuring 2cm (0.8in) on each side, and fitted into the space under black cocoa doughs.

STEPE
A triangular piece of black cocoa dough (frozen) measuring 2cm (0.8in) wide and 1.5cm (0.6in) high.

- ● Black: Black cocoa (about 105g / 3.7oz)
  - ★ Butter dough .... 53g / 1.87oz
  - ♥ Cake flour .... 37g / 1.31oz
  - Almond flour .... 7g / 0.25oz
  - Black cocoa powder .... 5g / 0.18oz
  - Cocoa powder .... 3g / 0.11oz
- ○ White: Plain (about 155g / 5.47oz)
  - ★ Butter dough .... 78g / 2.75oz
  - ♥ Cake flour .... 63g / 2.22oz
  - Almond flour .... 14g / 0.49oz

METHOD

1 Use the ★ ingredients to make the butter dough. (See p. 64.)
2 Add the ♥ ingredients to make up the four different colored doughs.

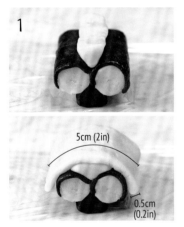

1

5cm (2in)

0.5cm (0.2in)

Make up the nose and mouth parts (see p. 74) and place a sheet of plain dough (room temperature) measuring 5cm (2in) wide and 0.5cm (0.2in) thick, on top. Ensure everything sticks together.
⇒Freeze for 15 mins.

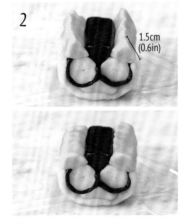

2

1.5cm (0.6in)

Place two triangular pieces of pumpkin dough (room temperature) measuring 1.5cm (0.6in) on each side, on top of step 1. Fill in any gaps and ensure everything sticks together.
⇒Freeze for 15 mins.

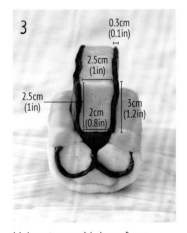

3

0.3cm (0.1in)

2.5cm (1in)

2.5cm (1in)

3cm (1.2in)

2cm (0.8in)

Make a trapezoid shape from pumpkin dough (frozen) with one side measuring 2cm (0.8in) across and the other parallel side measuring 2.5cm (1in) and 2.5cm (1in) high. Sandwich this between two sheets of black cocoa dough (room temperature) measuring 3cm (1.2in) wide and 0.3cm (0.1in) thick. Place all of this on top of step 2.
⇒Freeze for 15 – 20 mins.

4

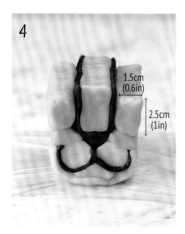

1.5cm
(0.6in)

2.5cm
(1in)

Attach two square-shaped pieces of pumpkin dough (room temperature) measuring 1.5cm (0.6in) wide and 2.5cm (1in) high to the sides of step 3. Ensure everything sticks together.

5

Make the parts for the eyes (see p. 74) and place them on top of step 4. Fill in any gaps.
⇒Freeze for 15–20 mins.

6

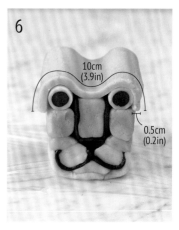

10cm
(3.9in)

0.5cm
(0.2in)

Place a sheet of pumpkin dough (room temperature) measuring 10cm (3.9in) wide and 0.5cm (0.2in) thick on top of step 5. Ensure everything sticks together.
⇒Freeze for 15 mins.

7

14cm
(5.5in)

0.5cm
(0.2in)

Place a sheet of cocoa dough (room temperature) measuring 14cm (5.5in) wide and 0.5cm (0.2in) thick on top of step 6. Ensure everything sticks together.

8

Make two parts for the ears (see p. 73). Attach them to the top of step 7. Ensure they stick on properly.
⇒Freeze for 15–20 mins.

9

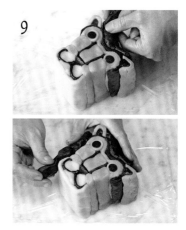

Attach 300g (10.6oz) of cocoa dough (room temperature) to the outer edges of step 8. Ensure everything sticks together.

Attach dough to the outer edges of step 9 to fill in any gaps. The Lion is finished after fixing up the overall shape.
⇒Freeze for 30 mins or longer.

Cut into 0.7–0.8cm (0.3in) thick slices and bake for 15 mins in an oven preheated to 170°C/338°F, then lower the temperature to 160°C/320°F and finish by baking for another 8–10 mins.

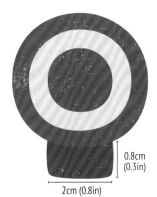

0.8cm
(0.3in)

2cm (0.8in)

TREE

Simply by attaching a block to the tree ring motif, you can easily make a tree design. It goes well with animal motif cookies.

INGREDIENTS

Ingredients
★Butter dough (about 80g / 2.82oz)
　Unsalted butter .... 40g / 1.41oz
　Powdered sugar ...... 30g / 1.06oz
　Whole egg .... 11g / 0.39oz
　1 pinch of salt
●Green: Matcha (about 100g / 3.53oz)
　★Butter dough .... 50g / 1.76oz
　♥Cake flour ....37g / 1.31oz
　　Almond flour .... 7g / 0.25oz
　　Matcha powder .... 6g / 0.21oz
○White: Plain (about 40g / 1.41oz)
　★Butter dough .... 20g / 0.71oz
　♥Cake flour .... 16g / 0.56oz
　　Almond flour ....4g / 0.14oz
●Brown: Cocoa (about 20g / 0.71oz)
　★Butter dough .... 10g / 0.35oz
　♥Cake flour .... 7g / 0.25oz
　　Almond flour .... 2g / 0.07oz
　　Cocoa powder.......... 2g / 0.07oz

METHOD

1　On top of the sheet of plain dough (room temperature) 8cm (3.1in) wide and 0.5cm (0.2in) thick, place a cylindrical piece of matcha dough (frozen) with a diameter of 2cm (0.8in). Wrap the plain dough around the matcha dough and roll it into shape.

2　Wrap a sheet of matcha dough (room temperature) 11cm (4.3in) wide and 0.5cm (0.2in) thick, around step 1. Wrap the matcha dough so that it totally encircles step 1. Cut off the leftover section with a knife and smooth over the cut surface.

3　Attach a square-shaped piece of cocoa dough (room temperature) measuring 2cm (0.8in) wide and 0.8cm (0.3in) high to the bottom of step 2.

4　Cut into 0.7–0.8cm (0.3in) thick slices and bake for 15 mins in an oven preheated to 170°C/338°F, then lower the temperature to 160°C/320°F and finish by baking for another 3 mins.
　*For steps 1 and 2, see p. 12 Tree Ring Motif, for the method.

INGREDIENTS

★Butter dough (about 200g / 7.05oz)
Unsalted butter............. 100g / 3.53oz
Powdered sugar .... 75g / 2.65oz
Whole egg......................... 27g / 0.95oz
2 pinches of salt

●Gray: Black sesame
(about 280g / 9.88oz)
★Butter dough .... 140g / 4.94oz
♥Cake flour .... 100g / 3.53oz
Almond flour................. 20g / 0.71oz
Ground sesame (black)
.... 20g / 0.71oz
Black sesame paste ..... ¹/₂ teaspoon

●Black: Black cocoa (about 60g / 2.12oz)
★Butter dough .... 30g / 1.06oz
♥Cake flour .... 21g / 0.74oz
Almond flour..................... 4g / 0.14oz
Black cocoa powder........... 3g / 0.11oz
Cocoa powder .... 2g / 0.07oz

15

KOALA

MAKE THE BASIC PARTS   *All parts are 8cm (3.1in) in length.

EAR
Wrap a sheet of black sesame dough (room temperature) 7cm (2.8in) wide and 0.8cm (0.3in) thick around a semi-cylindrical piece of plain dough (frozen) measuring 1.5cm (0.6in) wide and 2cm (0.8in) high. Make two parts.

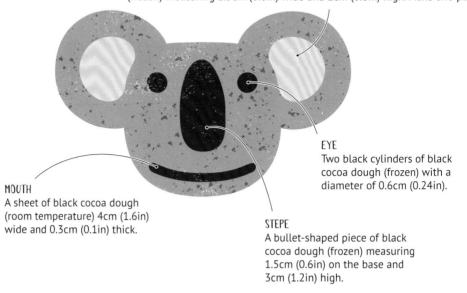

EYE
Two black cylinders of black cocoa dough (frozen) with a diameter of 0.6cm (0.24in).

MOUTH
A sheet of black cocoa dough (room temperature) 4cm (1.6in) wide and 0.3cm (0.1in) thick.

STEPE
A bullet-shaped piece of black cocoa dough (frozen) measuring 1.5cm (0.6in) on the base and 3cm (1.2in) high.

White: Plain (about 60g / 2.12oz)
★Butter dough ....30g / 1.06oz
♥Cake flour..........................25g / 0.88oz
  Almond flour.......................5g / 0.18oz

* Depending on the person who makes it, the size
  of the parts may vary so the amounts for the
  ingredients are on the generous side.

METHOD

1 Use the ★ ingredients to make the
  butter dough. (See p. 64.)
2 Add the ♥ ingredients to make up
  the three different colored doughs.

1

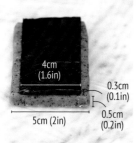

Place a sheet of black cocoa dough
(room temperature) measuring
4cm (1.6in) wide and 0.3cm (0.1in)
thick on top of a sheet of black
sesame dough (frozen) measuring
5cm (2in) wide and 0.5cm (0.2in)
thick.

2

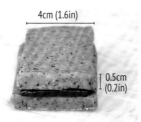

Place a sheet of black sesame
dough (frozen) 4cm (1.6in) wide
and 0.5cm (0.2in) thick on top of
step 1.

3

Place a bullet-shaped piece
of black cocoa dough (frozen)
measuring 1.5cm (0.6in) on the
base and 3cm (1.2in) high, on top
of step 2.
⇒Freeze for 15 mins.

4

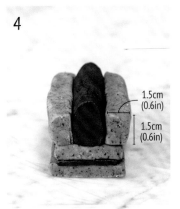

1.5cm
(0.6in)

1.5cm
(0.6in)

Attach two square-shaped pieces of black sesame dough (room temperature) measuring 1.5cm (0.6in) on each side, to either side of step 3. Ensure everything sticks together well.

5

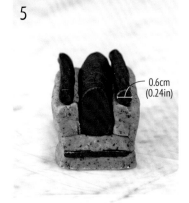

0.6cm
(0.24in)

Place two cylinders of black cocoa dough (frozen) with a diameter of 0.6cm (0.24in) on top of step 4.
⇒Freeze for 5 mins.

6

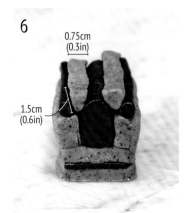

0.75cm
(0.3in)

1.5cm
(0.6in)

Cut in half a triangular piece of black sesame dough (room temperature) measuring 1.5cm (0.6in) on each side. Place these two triangular pieces inside the gaps of step 5 and ensure that everything sticks together.
⇒Freeze for 5 mins.

7

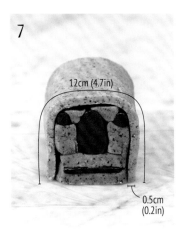

12cm (4.7in)

0.5cm
(0.2in)

Cover step 6 with a sheet of black sesame dough (room temperature) 12cm (4.7in) wide and 0.5cm (0.2in) thick.

8

Turn step 7 upside down and ensure the parts stick to each other. Fix up the shape too.
⇒Freeze for 15–20 mins.

9

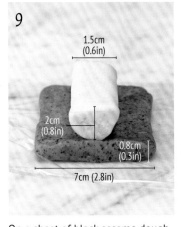

1.5cm
(0.6in)

2cm
(0.8in)

0.8cm
(0.3in)

7cm (2.8in)

On a sheet of black sesame dough (room temperature) measuring 7cm (2.8in) wide and 0.8cm (0.3in) thick, place a semi-cylindrical piece of plain dough (frozen) measuring 1.5cm (0.6in) at the base and 2cm (0.8in) high, upside down.

10

Slowly wrap the sheet around
the cylinder and ensure it sticks
together. Make two of these.

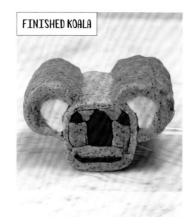

Attach the two parts from step
10 to the head of the koala and
ensure they are firmly stuck on.
⇒Freeze for 30 mins or longer.

Cut into 0.7–0.8cm (0.3in) thick slices
and bake for 15 mins in an oven
preheated to 170°C/338°F, then lower
the temperature to 160°C/320°F and
finish by baking for another 5–8 mins.

★Butter dough (about 260g / 9.17oz)
Unsalted butter............130g / 4.59oz
Powdered sugar ....99g / 3.49oz
Whole egg...........................34g / 1.2oz
3 pinches of salt

●Brown: Cocoa (about 250g / 8.82oz)
★Butter dough ....125g / 4.41oz
♥Cake flour ....90g / 3.17oz
Almond flour.....................18g / 0.63oz
Cocoa powder ....17g / 0.6oz

●Beige: Kinako (about 160g / 5.64oz)
★Butter dough ....80g / 2.82oz
♥Cake flour ....58g / 2.05oz
Kinako.................................11g / 0.39oz
Almond flour.....................11g / 0.39oz

* Depending on the person who makes it, the size
   of the parts may vary so the amounts for the
   ingredients are on the generous side.

16

OWL

MAKE THE BASIC PARTS   *All parts are 8cm (3.1in) in length.

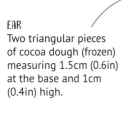

EAR
Two triangular pieces
of cocoa dough (frozen)
measuring 1.5cm (0.6in)
at the base and 1cm
(0.4in) high.

EYE
Make an eye by wrapping a
sheet of plain dough (room
temperature) 5cm (2in) wide
and 0.2cm (0.1in) thick,
around a cylinder of black
cocoa dough (frozen) with a
diameter of 1cm (0.4in). Make
two of these parts.

BEAK
One triangular piece of pumpkin
dough (room temperature)
measuring 1cm (0.4in) on each
side, was combined with another
triangular piece of pumpkin
dough (frozen) measuring 1.5cm
(0.6in) on each side.

- ● Black: Black cocoa (about 60g / 2.12oz)
- ★ Butter dough ....30g / 1.06oz
- ♥ Cake flour ....21g / 0.74oz
  - Almond flour........................4g / 0.14oz
  - Black cocoa powder...........3g / 0.11oz
  - Cocoa powder ....2g / 0.07oz

- ○ White: Plain (about 30g / 1.06oz)
- ★ Butter dough .... 15g / 0.53oz
- ♥ Cake flour .... 12g / 0.42oz
  - Almond flour....................3g / 0.11oz

- ● Yellow: Pumpkin (about 20g / 0.71oz)
- ★ Butter dough ....10g / 0.35oz
- ♥ Cake flour ....7g / 0.25oz
  - Almond flour........................2g / 0.07oz
  - Pumpkin powder................2g / 0.07oz

METHOD

1 Use the ★ ingredients to make the butter dough. (See p. 64.)
2 Add the ♥ ingredients to make up the five different colored doughs.

1

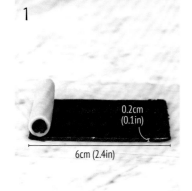

0.2cm (0.1in)

6cm (2.4in)

Make two of the parts for the eyes (see p. 74) and wrap each part in a sheet of black cocoa dough (room temperature) measuring 6cm (2.4in) wide and 0.2cm (0.1in) thick.

2

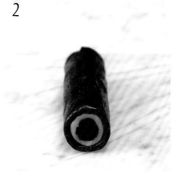

The eye part wrapped in black cocoa dough. Smooth over the cut edge.
⇒Freeze for 15 mins.

3

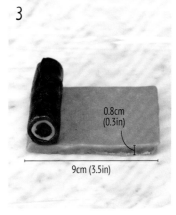

0.8cm (0.3in)

9cm (3.5in)

Wrap the eye part from step 2 in a sheet of kinako dough (room temperature) 9cm (3.5in) wide and 0.8cm (0.3in) thick.

4

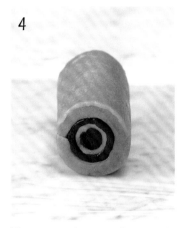

The eye part from step 3 wrapped in the kinako dough. Smooth over the cut edge. Make two of these.
⇒Freeze for 15 mins.

5

1cm (0.4in)

Insert a triangular piece of pumpkin dough (room temperature) between the two eye parts of step 4. Ensure it all sticks together.

6

1cm
(0.4in)

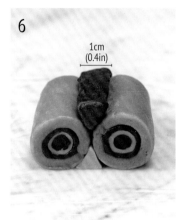

Place a triangular piece of cocoa dough (room temperature) measuring 1cm (0.4in) on each side on top of step 5.

7

Press the cocoa dough with your fingers and spread it out, ensuring it all sticks together.
⇒Freeze for 15 mins.

8

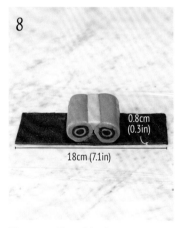

0.8cm
(0.3in)

18cm (7.1in)

Place step 7 upside down on a sheet of cocoa dough measuring 18cm (7.1in) wide and 0.8cm (0.3in) thick.

9

1.5cm
(0.6in)

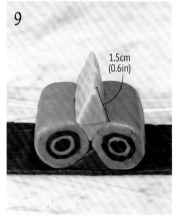

Attach a triangular piece of kinako dough (frozen) measuring 1.5cm (0.6in) wide on each side, to the top of step 8. Ensure it all sticks together.

10

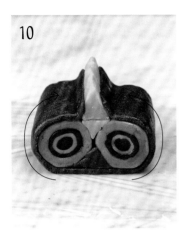

Wrap the sheet of cocoa dough from step 9 up around the eye parts and ensure it all sticks together.
⇒Freeze for 15–20 mins.

11

3.5cm (1.4in)

1cm (0.4in)

2.5cm (1in)

Place two trapezoid-shaped pieces of cocoa dough (room temperature) measuring 3.5cm (1.4in) at the base and 2.5cm (1in) on the parallel side, on either side of step 10.

12

Press the cocoa dough with your fingers so that it spreads out and covers the yellow beak part, filling in any gaps.
⇒Freeze for 15–20 mins.

FINISHED OWL

1cm (0.4in)

1.5cm (0.6in)

Turn step 12 the right side up again and attach two triangular pieces of cocoa dough (frozen) on either side. The Owl is finished after ensuring everything sticks together well.
⇒Freeze for 30 mins or longer.

Cut into 0.7–0.8cm (0.3in) thick slices and bake for 15 mins in an oven preheated to 170°C/338°F, then lower the temperature to 160°C/320°F and finish by baking for another 5–8 mins.

★Butter dough (about 220g / 7.76oz)
Unsalted butter............110g / 3.88oz
Powdered sugar.............82g / 2.89oz
Whole egg.......................30g / 1.06oz
2 pinches of salt

⚪White: Plain (about 340g / 12oz)
★Butter dough ....170g / 6oz
♥Cake flour ....140g / 4.94oz
Almond flour.....................30g / 1.06oz

* Depending on the person who makes it, the size
of the parts may vary so the amounts for the
ingredients are on the generous side.

⚫Black: Black cocoa (about 70g / 2.47oz)
★Butter dough ....35g / 1.23oz
♥Cake flour ....25g / 0.88oz
Almond flour.......................5g / 0.18oz
Black cocoa powder...........4g / 0.14oz
Cocoa powder ....2g / 0.07oz

17

POLAR BEAR

MAKE THE BASIC PARTS *All parts are 8cm (3.1in) in length.

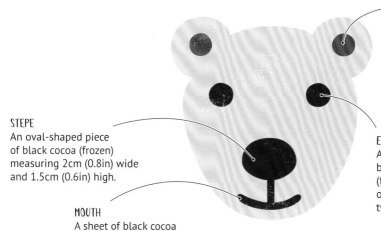

EAR
Make an ear by wrapping a
sheet of plain dough (room
temperature) measuring 3cm
(1.2in) wide and 0.5cm (0.2in)
thick, around a cylindrical piece
of purple sweet potato dough
(frozen) with a diameter of 0.8cm
(0.3in). Make two of these parts.

STEPE
An oval-shaped piece
of black cocoa (frozen)
measuring 2cm (0.8in) wide
and 1.5cm (0.6in) high.

EYE
A cylindrical piece of
black cocoa dough
(frozen) with a diameter
of 0.8cm (0.3in). Make
two of these parts.

MOUTH
A sheet of black cocoa
dough (frozen) measuring
2.5cm (1in) wide and 0.3cm
(0.1in) thick.

METHOD

1 Use the ★ ingredients to make the butter dough. (See p. 64.)
2 Add the ♥ ingredients to make up the three different colored doughs.

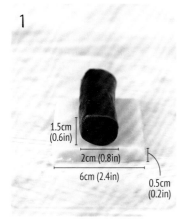

1

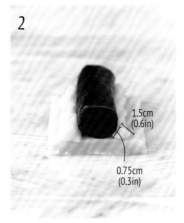

2

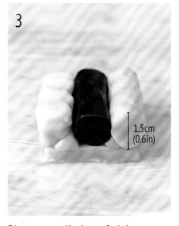

3

Place a cylindrical piece of black cocoa dough (frozen) measuring 2cm (0.8in) wide and 1.5cm (0.6in) high on top of a sheet of plain dough (frozen) 6cm (2.4in) wide and 0.5cm (0.2in) thick.

Cut in half a triangular piece of plain dough (frozen) measuring 1.5cm (0.6in) on each side so that one side measures 0.75cm (0.3in). Place these two pieces on the sides of step 1. Fill in any gaps and ensure the pieces stick together.

Place two cylinders of plain dough (room temperature) with a diameter of 1.5cm (0.6in) on top of step 2. Fill in any gaps and ensure the pieces stick together.
⇒Freeze for 15 mins.

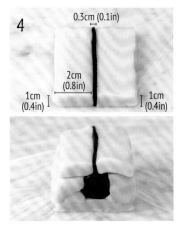

4

0.3cm (0.1in)

2cm (0.8in)

1cm (0.4in)   1cm (0.4in)

Sandwich a piece of black cocoa dough (frozen) measuring 0.3cm (0.1in) thick, between two sheets of plain dough (room temperature) 2cm (0.8in) wide and 1cm (0.4in) thick. Place on top of step 3. Ensure everything sticks together.
⇒Freeze for 15–20 mins.

5

2.5cm (1in)

0.3cm (0.1in)

Place a sheet of black cocoa dough (frozen) 2.5cm (1in) wide and 0.3cm (0.1in) thick on top of step 4.

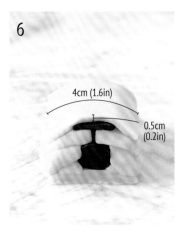

6

4cm (1.6in)

0.5cm (0.2in)

Cover step 5 with a sheet of plain dough (room temperature) 4cm (1.6in) wide and 0.5cm (0.2in) thick. Ensure everything sticks together.
⇒Freeze for 15–20 mins.

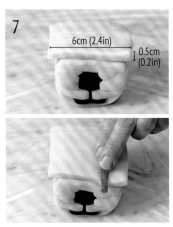

7

6cm (2.4in)

0.5cm (0.2in)

Turn step 6 upside down and place a sheet of plain dough (room temperature) measuring 6cm (2.4in) wide and 0.5cm (0.2in) thick on top. Use a chopstick to make depressions on both sides.

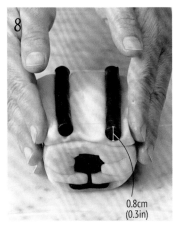

8

0.8cm (0.3in)

Place cylindrical pieces of cocoa dough (frozen) with a diameter of 0.8cm (0.3in), in the depressions created in step 7. Fill in the gaps around the cylinders of cocoa dough.
⇒Freeze for 15 mins.

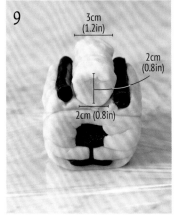

9

3cm (1.2in)

2cm (0.8in)

2cm (0.8in)

Place a trapezoid-shaped piece of plain dough (room temperature) measuring 3cm (1.2in) at the base and 2cm (0.8in) on the parallel side, on top of step 8.

10

Push step 9 with your fingers so that the piece of plain dough spreads out and covers the eyes.
⇒Freeze for 15–20 mins.

11

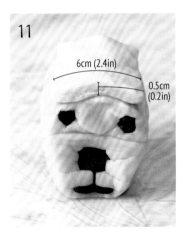

6cm (2.4in)

0.5cm (0.2in)

Cover step 10 with a sheet of plain dough (room temperature) measuring 6cm (2.4in) wide and 0.5cm (0.2in) thick. Ensure that everything sticks together and fix up the shape.
⇒Freeze for 15–20 mins.

12

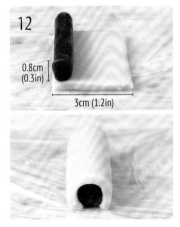

0.8cm (0.3in)

3cm (1.2in)

Wrap a cylindrical piece of purple sweet potato dough (frozen) with a diameter of 0.8cm (0.3in), in a sheet of plain dough (room temperature) 3cm (1.2in) and 0.5cm (0.2in) thick. Make two of these parts.
⇒Freeze for 5 mins.

FINISHED POLAR BEAR

Attach step 12 to step 11 firmly. The Polar Bear is finished after ensuring that all the parts stick together well.
⇒Freeze for 30 mins or longer.

Cut into 0.7–0.8cm (0.3in) thick slices and bake for 15 mins in an oven preheated to 170°C/338°F, then lower the temperature to 160°C/320°F and finish by baking for another 5–8 mins.

★Butter dough (about 260g / 9.17oz)
Unsalted butter.............130g / 4.59oz
Powdered sugar ....99g / 3.49oz
Whole egg...........................34g / 1.2oz
3 pinches of salt

●Black: Black cocoa
(about 280g / 9.88oz)
★Butter dough ....140g / 4.94oz
♥Cake flour ....98g / 3.46oz
Almond flour.....................21g / 0.74oz
Black cocoa powder.........14g / 0.49oz
Cocoa powder ....7g / 0.25oz

●White: Plain (about 220g / 7.76oz)
★Butter dough ....110g / 3.88oz
♥Cake flour ....90g / 3.17oz
Almond flour.....................20g / 0.71oz

* Depending on the person who makes it, the size
of the parts may vary so the amounts for the
ingredients are on the generous side.

18

PENGUIN

MAKE THE BASIC PARTS   *All parts are 8cm (3.1in) in length.

EYE
Two cylinders of black
cocoa dough (frozen) with a
diameter of 0.5cm (0.2in).

BEAK
A square-shaped piece
of pumpkin dough with
one side measuring
0.8cm (0.3in).

● Yellow: Pumpkin (about 20g / 0.71oz)
★ Butter dough .... 10g / 0.35oz
♥ Cake flour .... 7g / 0.25oz
　Almond flour........................ 2g / 0.07oz
　Pumpkin powder................ 2g / 0.07oz

METHOD

1　Use the ★ ingredients to make the butter dough. (See p. 64.)
2　Add the ♥ ingredients to make up the three different colored doughs.

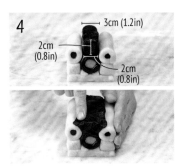

1

Cut a triangular piece of plain dough (room temperature) with one side measuring 1.5cm (0.6in) in half and place them on top of a sheet of plain dough (frozen) measuring 7cm (2.8in) wide and 1cm (0.4in) thick.

2

Wrap a sheet of black cocoa dough (room temperature) around a square-shaped piece of pumpkin dough (frozen). Place this on top of step 1 and ensure everything sticks together.
⇒Freeze for 15–20 mins.

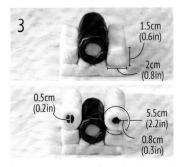

3

Place two square-shaped pieces of plain dough (room temperature) on step 2. Wrap two cylinders of black cocoa dough (frozen) in sheets of plain dough (room temperature). Place them as in the photo.
⇒Freeze for 15–20 mins.

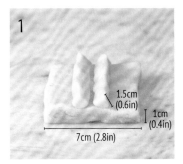

4

Place a trapezoid-shaped piece of cocoa dough (room temperature) measuring 2cm (0.8in) at the base and 3cm (1.2in) on the parallel side, on top of step 3. Press the cocoa dough with your fingers so that it spreads out and all sticks together.
⇒Freeze for 15–20 mins.

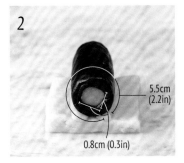

5

Place a sheet of black cocoa dough (room temperature) 4cm (1.6in) wide and 1cm (0.4in) thick on top of step 4 and fix up the overall shape.

FINISHED PENGUIN

Place a sheet of black cocoa dough (room temperature) over step 5. The Penguin is finished after the overall shape is fixed up and then ensuring that all the parts stick together well.
⇒Freeze for 30 mins or longer.

Cut into 0.7–0.8cm (0.3in) thick slices and bake for 15 mins in an oven preheated to 170°C/338°F, then lower the temperature to 160°C/320°F and finish by baking for another 5–8 mins.

★Butter dough (about 220g / 7.76oz)
Unsalted butter............110g / 3.88oz
Powdered sugar.............82g / 2.89oz
Whole egg.......................30g / 1.06oz
2 pinches of salt

●Purple: Purple sweet potato
(about 260g / 9.17oz)
★Butter dough .... 130g / 4.59oz
♥Cake flour ....94g / 3.32oz
Almond flour....................18g / 0.63oz
Purple sweet potato powder
....18g / 0.63oz

●Yellow: Pumpkin (about 130g / 4.59oz)
★Butter dough ....65g / 2.29oz
♥Cake flour ....47g / 1.66oz
Almond flour......................9g / 0.32oz
Pumpkin powder...............9g / 0.32oz

* Depending on the person who makes it, the size of the parts may vary so the amounts for the ingredients are on the generous side.

19

MASKED WRESTLER
(MASKED)

MAKE THE BASIC PARTS
*All parts are 8cm (3.1in) in length.

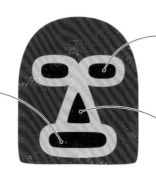

EYE
Make an eye by wrapping a sheet of pumpkin dough (room temperature) 5.5cm (2.2in) wide and 0.5cm (0.2in) thick, around a cylinder of black cocoa dough (frozen) with a diameter of 1.2cm (0.5in). Make two of these parts.

MOUTH
Wrap a sheet of pumpkin dough (room temperature) 7.5cm (3in) wide and 0.5cm (0.2in) thick, around an oval-shaped piece of black cocoa dough (frozen) measuring 3cm (1.2in) wide and 0.5cm (0.2in) high.

STEPE
Wrap a sheet of pumpkin dough (room temperature) 5cm (2in) wide and 0.5cm (0.2in) thick, around a triangular piece of black cocoa dough (frozen) measuring 1cm (0.4in) on each side.

- ●Black: Black cocoa (about 55g / 1.94oz)
- ★Butter dough .... 23g / 0.81oz
- ♥Cake flour .... 16g / 0.56oz
  - Almond flour .... 3g / 0.11oz
  - Black cocoa powder .... 11g / 0.39oz

METHOD

1. Use the ★ ingredients to make the butter dough. (See p. 64.)
2. Add the ♥ ingredients to make up the three different colored doughs.

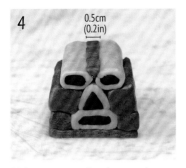

1

7.5cm (3in)
0.5cm (0.2in)
0.5cm (0.2in)
3cm (1.2in)
0.5cm (0.2in)
5.5cm (2.2in)

Place the oval-shaped piece of black cocoa dough (frozen) that was wrapped in a sheet of pumpkin dough (room temperature), on top of a sheet of purple sweet potato dough (frozen).
⇒Freeze for 5 mins.

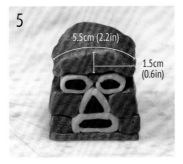

2

5cm (2in)
0.5cm (0.2in)
1cm (0.4in)

On top of step 1, place a triangular piece of black cocoa dough (frozen) measuring 1cm (0.4in) on each side and wrapped in a sheet of pumpkin dough (room temperature).
⇒Freeze for 5 mins.

3

1cm (0.4in)
2.5cm (1in)
1.5cm (0.6in)
2cm (0.8in)

Place two square-shaped pieces of purple sweet potato dough (room temperature) on step 2. Then on top of these, place two trapezoid-shaped pieces of purple sweet potato dough (room temperature). Ensure everything sticks together.

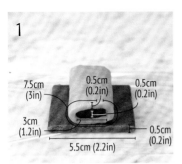

4

0.5cm (0.2in)

Make two parts for the eyes (see p. 74). Place these parts on top of step 3. Insert a triangular piece of purple sweet potato dough (room temperature) between the two eyes. Fill in any gaps and ensure everything sticks together.
⇒Freeze for 15–20 mins.

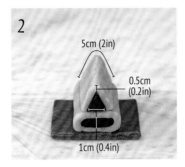

5

5.5cm (2.2in)
1.5cm (0.6in)

Place a semi-cylindrical piece of purple sweet potato dough (room temperature) measuring 5.5cm (2.2in) at the base and 1.5cm (0.6in) high, on top of step 4.

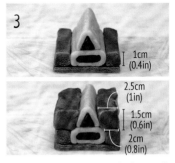

FINISHED MASKED WRESTLER

Press the purple sweet potato dough with your fingers so that it spreads out and fills any gaps. The Masked Wrestler is finished after fixing up the overall shape.
⇒Freeze for 30 mins or longer.

Cut into 0.7–0.8cm (0.3in) thick slices and bake for 15 mins in an oven preheated to 170°C/338°F, then lower the temperature to 160°C/320°F and finish by baking for another 5–8 mins.

★Butter dough (about 180g / 6.35oz)
Unsalted butter...............90g / 3.17oz
Powdered sugar ....68g / 2.4oz
Whole egg.......................24g / 0.85oz
2 pinches of salt

●Green: Matcha (about 155g / 5.47oz)
★Butter dough ....78g / 2.75oz
♥Cake flour ....57g / 2.01oz
  Almond flour....................11g / 0.39oz
  Matcha powder ....9g / 0.32oz

●Yellow: Pumpkin (about 155g / 5.47oz)
★Butter dough ....78g / 2.75oz
♥Cake flour ....56g / 1.98oz
  Almond flour....................11g / 0.39oz
  Pumpkin powder.............11g / 0.39oz

* Depending on the person who makes it, the size
  of the parts may vary so the amounts for the
  ingredients are on the generous side.

19

MASKED WRESTLER
(HALF AND HALF)

MAKE THE BASIC PARTS

*All parts are 8cm (3.1in) in length.

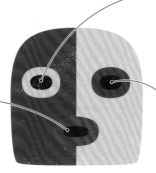

RIGHT EYE
Wrap a sheet of pumpkin dough (room temperature) 4cm (1.6in) wide and 0.3cm (0.1in) thick, around an oval-shaped piece of black cocoa dough (frozen) measuring 1cm (0.4in) wide and 0.8cm (0.3in) high.

LEFT EYE
Wrap a sheet of matcha dough (room temperature) 4cm (1.6in) wide and 0.3cm (0.1in) thick, around an oval-shaped piece of black cocoa dough (frozen) measuring 1cm (0.4in) wide and 0.8cm (0.3in) high.

MOUTH
Wrap a sheet of purple sweet potato dough (room temperature) 5cm (2in) wide and 0.3cm (0.1in) thick, around an oval-shaped piece of black cocoa dough (frozen) measuring 1.5cm (0.6in) wide and 0.5cm (0.2in) high.

- ● Black: Black cocoa (about 25g / 0.88oz)
- ★ Butter dough ....13g / 0.46oz
- ♥ Cake flour ....9g / 0.32oz
  Almond flour........................ 2g / 0.07oz
  Black cocoa powder........... 2g / 0.07oz

- ● Purple: Purple sweet potato (about 20g / 0.71oz)
- ★ Butter dough ....10g / 0.35oz
- ♥ Cake flour ....7g / 0.25oz
  Almond flour...................2g / 0.07oz
  Purple sweet potato powder
  ....2g / 0.07oz

METHOD

1. Use the ★ ingredients to make the butter dough. (See p. 64.)
2. Add the ♥ ingredients to make up the four different colored doughs.

1

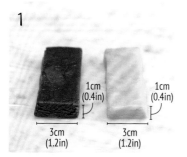

1cm (0.4in)
1cm (0.4in)
3cm (1.2in)
3cm (1.2in)

Make sheets of matcha and pumpkin doughs (frozen), both measuring 3cm (1.2in) wide and 1cm (0.4in) thick.

2

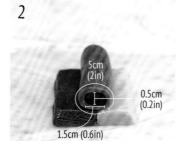

5cm (2in)
0.5cm (0.2in)
1.5cm (0.6in)

Combine the two sheets of doughs ensuring they stick together well. Wrap a sheet of purple sweet potato dough (room temperature) around an oval-shaped piece of black cocoa dough (frozen). Place this on the combined sheets. ⇒Freeze for 5 mins.

3

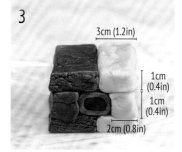

3cm (1.2in)
1cm (0.4in)
1cm (0.4in)
2cm (0.8in)

Place a square-shaped piece each of matcha and pumpkin dough (room temperature) on top of step 2. Then place one piece each of matcha dough and pumpkin dough (room temperature). Ensure everything sticks together.

4

0.5cm (0.2in)
1cm (0.4in)

Make up the two different parts for the eyes (see p. 74) by wrapping sheets of pumpkin and matcha doughs (room temperature) around oval-shaped piece of black cocoa dough (frozen). Place the eyes on top of step 3.
⇒Freeze for 15–20 mins.

5

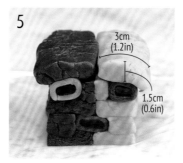

3cm (1.2in)
1.5cm (0.6in)

Make fan-shaped pieces from matcha and pumpkin dough (room temperature) measuring 3cm (1.2in) wide and 1.5cm (0.6in) high. Please these on top of step 4.

FINISHED MASKED WRESTLER

Push with your fingers so that the doughs spread out and cover the sides of the eyes. The Masked Wrestler is finished after fixing up the overall shape.
⇒Freeze for 30 mins or longer.

Cut into 0.7–0.8cm (0.3in) thick slices and bake for 15 mins in an oven preheated to 170°C/338°F, then lower the temperature to 160°C/320°F and finish by baking for another 5–8 mins.

★Butter dough (about 155g / 5.47oz)
Unsalted butter...............78g / 2.75oz
Powdered sugar ....59g / 2.08oz
Whole egg.........................20g / 0.71oz
1 pinch of salt

⚪White: Plain (about 220g / 7.76oz)
★Butter dough ....110g / 3.88oz
♥Cake flour ....90g / 3.17oz
Almond flour....................20g / 0.71oz

* Depending on the person who makes it, the size
of the parts may vary so the amounts for the
ingredients are on the generous side.

●Red: Raspberry (about 70g / 2.47oz)
★Butter dough ....35g / 1.23oz
♥Cake flour ....26g / 0.92oz
Almond flour.......................5g / 0.18oz
Raspberry powder ....4g / 0.14oz

19

MASKED WRESTLER
(TRIANGULAR)

MAKE THE BASIC PARTS   *All parts are 8cm (3.1in) in length.

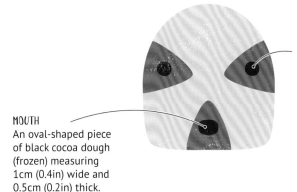

EYE
Two cylinders of black
cocoa dough (frozen)
with a diameter of
0.5cm (0.2in).

MOUTH
An oval-shaped piece
of black cocoa dough
(frozen) measuring
1cm (0.4in) wide and
0.5cm (0.2in) thick.

● Black: Black cocoa (about 20g / 0.71oz)
★ Butter dough ....10g / 0.35oz
♥ Cake flour ....7g / 0.25oz
　 Almond flour......................2g / 0.07oz
　 Black cocoa powder...........2g / 0.07oz

METHOD

1　Use the ★ ingredients to make the butter dough. (See p. 64.)
2　Add the ♥ ingredients to make up the three different colored doughs.

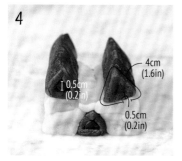

1

1cm (0.4in)
0.5cm (0.2in)
4cm (1.6in)
0.5cm (0.2in)

Wrap an oval-shaped piece of black cocoa dough (frozen), with a sheet of raspberry dough (room temperature). Make it into a triangular shape and ensure everything sticks together.
⇒Freeze for 15 mins.

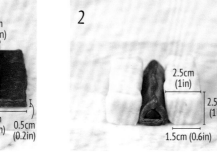

2

2.5cm (1in)
2.5cm (1in)
1.5cm (0.6in)

On either side of step 1 place trapezoid-shaped pieces of plain dough (room temperature) measuring 1.5cm (0.6in) at the base and 2.5cm (1in) high.
⇒Freeze for 15 mins.

3

1.5cm (0.6in)
2cm (0.8in)

Place two triangular pieces of plain dough (room temperature) measuring 2cm (0.8in) at the base and 1.5cm (0.6in) high. Ensure everything sticks together.

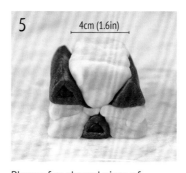

4

4cm (1.6in)
0.5cm (0.2in)
0.5cm (0.2in)

Wrap two cylindrical pieces of black cocoa dough (frozen) with a diameter 0.5cm (0.2in), with sheets of raspberry dough (room temperature). Make them into triangular shapes and freeze for 15 mins. Then place on top of step 3.
⇒Freeze for 15 mins.

5

4cm (1.6in)

Place a fan-shaped piece of plain dough (room temperature) measuring 4cm (1.6in) at the top, on top of step 4.

FINISHED MASKED WRESTER

The Masked Wrestler is finished after you make everything in step 5 stick together and finish off the overall shape.
⇒Freeze for 30 mins or longer.

Cut into 0.7–0.8cm (0.3in) thick slices and bake for 15 mins in an oven preheated to 170°C/338°F, then lower the temperature to 160°C/320°F and finish by baking for another 5–8 mins.

★Butter dough (about 175g / 6.17oz)
Unsalted butter...............86g / 3.03oz
Powdered sugar ....66g / 2.33oz
Whole egg.........................23g / 0.81oz
2 pinches of salt

●Brown: Cocoa (about 225g / 7.94oz)
★Butter dough ....128g / 4.52oz
♥Cake flour ....92g / 3.25oz
Almond flour...................18g / 0.63oz
Cocoa powder ....18g / 0.63oz

○White: Plain (about 65g / 2.29oz)
★Butter dough ....33g / 1.16oz
♥Cake flour ....27g / 0.95oz
Almond flour......................6g / 0.21oz

* Depending on the person who makes it, the size
  of the parts may vary so the amounts for the
  ingredients are on the generous side.

20

CAKE

MAKE THE BASIC PARTS   *All parts are 8cm (3.1in) in length.

STRAWBERRIES
Three cylindrical pieces
of strawberry dough
(frozen) with a diameter
of 0.6cm (0.24in).

● Pink: Strawberry (about 25g / 0.88oz)
★ Butter dough .... 13g / 0.46oz
♥ Cake flour .... 9g / 0.32oz
　 Almond flour .... 2g / 0.07oz
　 Strawberry powder .... 2g / 0.07oz

METHOD

1 Use the ★ ingredients to make the butter dough. (See p. 64.)
2 Add the ♥ ingredients to make up the three different colored doughs.

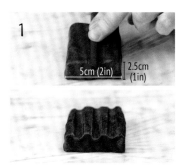

1

5cm (2in) 2.5cm (1in)

Use a chopstick to make three depressions in a square-shaped piece of cocoa dough (room temperature) measuring 5cm (2in) wide and 2.5cm (1in) high.

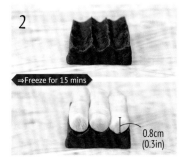

2

⇒Freeze for 15 mins

0.8cm (0.3in)

Improve the shape of the depressions from step 1 and freeze for 15 mins. Then place the three cylinders of plain dough (room temperature) with a diameter of 0.8cm (0.3in), in the three depressions of step 1.

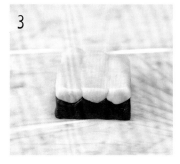

3

Ensure step 2 sticks together and then make the top of the part flat.
⇒Freeze for 15 mins.

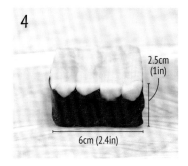

4

2.5cm (1in)

6cm (2.4in)

Using the same method as steps 1 and 2, make the bottom part with a square-shaped piece cocoa dough (room temperature). Place four cylinders of plain dough (room temperature) in the four depressions and make the top part flat.

5

Place step 3 on top of step 4.

FINISHED CAKE

Place three cylindrical pieces of strawberry dough (frozen) on top of step 5. The Cake is finished when everything is stuck together well.
⇒Freeze for 30 mins or longer.

Cut into 0.7–0.8cm (0.3in) thick slices and bake for 15 mins in an oven preheated to 170°C/338°F, then lower the temperature to 160°C/320°F and finish by baking for another 5–8 mins.

★Butter dough (about 220g / 7.76oz)
Unsalted butter.............110g / 3.88oz
Powdered sugar...............82g / 2.89oz
Whole egg.........................30g / 1.06oz
2 pinches of salt

● Yellow: Pumpkin (about 320g / 11.3oz)
★Butter dough.................160g / 5.64oz
♥ Cake flour......................115g / 4.06oz
Almond flour....................23g / 0.81oz
Pumpkin powder.............23g / 0.81oz

● Pink: Strawberry (about 70g / 2.47oz)
★Butter dough...................35g / 1.23oz
♥ Cake flour.........................25g / 0.88oz
Almond flour.......................5g / 0.18oz
Strawberry powder............6g / 0.21oz

* Depending on the person who makes it, the size of the parts may vary so the amounts for the ingredients are on the generous side.

21

PRESENT

MAKE THE BASIC PARTS
*All parts are 8cm (3.1in) in length.

RIBBON
A sheet of purple sweet potato dough (frozen) 5cm (2in) wide and 0.3cm (0.1in) thick, sandwiched between two sheets of strawberry dough (frozen) measuring 5cm (2in) wide and 0.3cm (0.1in) thick.

BOW
Three triangular pieces each of purple sweet potato dough and strawberry dough (frozen) measuring 1.5cm (0.6in) on each edge. Each piece is cut in half and the pieces are laid one on top of the other.

- **Purple: Purple sweet potato**
  (about 50g / 1.76oz)
- ★ Butter dough ....25g / 0.88oz
- ♥ Cake flour ....18g / 0.63oz
  Almond flour......................... 4g / 0.14oz
  Purple sweet potato powder
  ....3g / 0.11oz

METHOD

1 Use the ★ ingredients to make the butter dough. (See p. 64.)
2 Add the ♥ ingredients to make up the three different colored doughs.

1

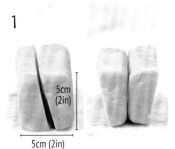

Cut diagonally a square-shaped piece of pumpkin dough (room temperature) measuring 5cm (2in) on each side. Turn one piece in the opposite direction.
⇒Freeze for 15 mins.

2

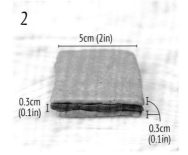

Sandwich a sheet of purple sweet potato dough (frozen) 5cm (2in) wide and 0.3cm (0.1in) thick, between two sheets of strawberry dough (frozen) 5cm (2in) wide and 0.3cm (0.1in) thick.

3

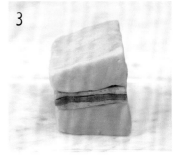

Sandwich step 2 between the two pieces of step 1. Ensure everything sticks together and fix up the overall shape.
⇒Freeze for 15–20 mins.

4

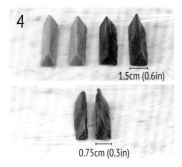

Cut in half three triangular pieces each of purple sweet potato dough and strawberry dough (frozen) measuring 1.5cm (0.6in) on each edge, to make three pieces of each color.

5

Lay the pieces from step 4 one on top of another and ensure they stick together.

FINISHED PRESENT

Place step 5 on top of step 3. The Present is finished after ensuring all the pieces stick together.
⇒Freeze for 30 mins or longer.

Cut into 0.7–0.8cm (0.3in) thick slices and bake for 15 mins in an oven preheated to 170°C/338°F, then lower the temperature to 160°C/320°F and finish by baking for another 5–8 mins.

INGREDIENTS

★Butter dough (about 225g / 7.94oz)
Unsalted butter ....128g / 4.52oz
Powdered sugar ....97g / 3.42oz
Whole egg.......................33g / 1.16oz
3 pinches of salt

●Yellow: Pumpkin (about 330g / 11.6oz)
(●Purple: Purple sweet potato)
★Butter dough ....165g / 5.82oz
♥Cake flour ....119g / 4.2oz
Almond flour................23g / 0.81oz
Pumpkin powder..........23g / 0.81oz
(Purple sweet potato powder)

●Black: Black cocoa (about 150g / 5.29oz)
★Butter dough ....75g / 2.65oz
♥Cake flour ....53g / 1.87oz
Almond flour....................10g / 0.35oz
Black cocoa powder...........8g / 0.28oz
Cocoa powder ....4g / 0.14oz

22

PUMPKIN

MAKE THE BASIC PARTS
*All parts are 8cm (3.1in) in length.

STEM
A square-shaped piece of matcha dough (room temperature) measuring 1.5cm (0.6in) wide and 1cm (0.4in) high.

NOSE
A triangular piece of black cocoa dough (frozen) with one side measuring 1.5cm (0.6in).

EYE
Two triangular pieces of black cocoa dough (frozen) with one side measuring 1.5cm (0.6in).

MOUTH
A semi-cylindrical piece of black cocoa (room temperature) measuring 5.5cm (2.2in) wide and 2cm (0.8in) high. Use a knife and chopstick to make the shape of this part.

- ● Green: Matcha (about 25g / 0.88oz)
- ★ Butter dough .... 13g / 0.46oz
- ♥ Cake flour .... 9g / 0.32oz
-   Almond flour........................ 2g / 0.07oz
-   Matcha powder .... 2g / 0.07oz

* Depending on the person who makes it, the size of the parts may vary so the amounts for the ingredients are on the generous side.

METHOD

1. Use the ★ ingredients to make the butter dough. (See p. 64.)
2. Add the ♥ ingredients to make up the three different colored doughs.

1

2cm (0.8in)

5.5cm (2.2in)

Make a semi-cylindrical piece of black cocoa dough (room temperature) 5.5cm (2.2in) wide and 2cm (0.8in) high. Make two cuts on the top and bottom sides. Then use a chopstick to make four square depressions.

2

0.6cm (0.24in)

In each depression, insert a cylindrical piece of pumpkin dough (room temperature) with a diameter of 0.6cm (0.24in). Ensure it sticks together well.
⇒Freeze for 15 mins.

3

5.5cm (2.2in)

0.8cm (0.3in) ⟶   0.8cm (0.3in)

13cm (5.1in)

Place a sheet of pumpkin dough (room temperature) on top of step 2. Place this all on top of a sheet of pumpkin dough (room temperature). Wrap the sheet around the center piece and ensure it all sticks together.
⇒Freeze for 15 mins.

4

1.5cm (0.6in)

2cm (0.8in)

Place three triangular pieces of black cocoa dough (frozen) on top of step 3. Then insert two triangular pieces of pumpkin dough (room temperature) in the gaps between the black cocoa dough. Ensure everything sticks together.
⇒Freeze for 5 mins.

5

10cm (3.9in)

0.8cm (0.3in)

Cover step 4 with a sheet of pumpkin dough (room temperature) measuring 10cm (3.9in) wide and 0.8cm (0.3in) thick. Ensure everything sticks together.

FINISHED PUMPKIN

1cm (0.4in)

1.5cm (0.6in)

Place a square-shaped piece of matcha dough (room temperature) on top of step 5. The Pumpkin is finished after ensuring everything sticks together well.
⇒Freeze for 30 mins or longer.

Cut into 0.7–0.8cm (0.3in) thick slices and bake for 15 mins in an oven preheated to 170°C/338°F, then lower the temperature to 160°C/320°F and finish by baking for another 5–8 mins.

★Butter dough (about 200g / 7.05oz)
  Unsalted butter............. 100g / 3.53oz
  Powdered sugar ....75g / 2.65oz
  Whole egg..........................27g / 0.95oz
  2 pinches of salt

●Purple: Purple sweet potato
  (about 330g / 11.6oz)
★Butter dough .... 165g / 5.82oz
♥Cake flour ....119g / 4.2oz
  Almond flour.....................23g / 0.81oz
  Purple sweet potato powder
  ....23g / 0.81oz

●Black: Black cocoa (about 45g / 1.59oz)
★Butter dough ....23g / 0.81oz
♥Cake flour ....16g / 0.56oz
  Almond flour.......................3g / 0.11oz
  Black cocoa powder...........4g / 0.14oz

* Depending on the person who makes it, the size of the parts may vary so the amounts for the ingredients are on the generous side.

23

WITCH'S HAT

MAKE THE BASIC PARTS   *All parts are 8cm (3.1in) in length.

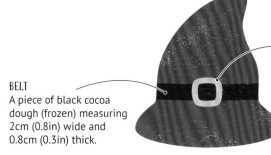

BELT
A piece of black cocoa dough (frozen) measuring 2cm (0.8in) wide and 0.8cm (0.3in) thick.

BUCKLE
A square-shaped piece of black cocoa dough (frozen) measuring 0.8cm (0.3in) on one side, wrapped in a sheet of pumpkin dough (room temperature) measuring 5cm (2in) wide and 0.3cm (0.1in) thick.

- 🔘 Yellow: Pumpkin (about 20g / 0.71oz)
- ★ Butter dough .... 10g / 0.35oz
- ♥ Cake flour .... 7g / 0.25oz
-    Almond flour .... 2g / 0.07oz
-    Pumpkin powder .... 2g / 0.07oz

METHOD

1 Use the ★ ingredients to make the butter dough. (See p. 64.)
2 Add the ♥ ingredients to make up the three different colored doughs.

1

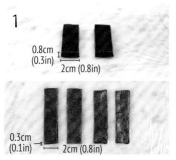

0.8cm (0.3in)
2cm (0.8in)

0.3cm (0.1in)
2cm (0.8in)

Make two bars of black cocoa dough (frozen) measuring 2cm (0.8in) wide and 0.8cm (0.3in) thick, and four pieces of purple sweet potato dough (room temperature) measuring 2cm (0.8in) wide and 0.3cm (0.1in) thick.

2

Sandwich a bar of black cocoa dough (frozen) between two pieces of purple sweet potato dough (room temperature). Make two of these parts.
⇒Freeze for 15 mins.

3

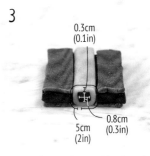

0.3cm (0.1in)

5cm (2in)
0.8cm (0.3in)

Wrap a sheet of pumpkin dough (room temperature) around a square-shaped piece of black cocoa dough (frozen). Sandwich this between the two parts from step 2.
⇒Freeze for 5 mins.

4

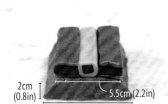

2cm (0.8in)
5.5cm (2.2in)
7cm (2.8in)

Make a trapezoid-shaped piece of purple sweet potato dough (room temperature). Place step 3 on top of this and push it down gently, ensuring everything sticks together.
⇒Freeze for 15–20 mins.

5

5cm (2in)

Make a triangular-shaped piece of purple sweet potato dough (room temperature) measuring 5cm (2in) on one side.

FINISHED WITCH'S HAT

Place step 5 on step 4. The Witch's Hat is finished after pushing the entire piece together gently to ensure that everything sticks together.
⇒Freeze for 30 mins or longer.

Cut into 0.7–0.8cm (0.3in) thick slices and bake for 15 mins in an oven preheated to 170°C/338°F, then lower the temperature to 160°C/320°F and finish by baking for another 5–8 mins.

★Butter dough (about 250g / 8.82oz)
  Unsalted butter............125g / 4.41oz
  Powdered sugar ....95g / 3.35oz
  Whole egg.......................33g / 1.16oz
  2 pinches of salt

●Purple: Purple sweet potato
  (about 300g / 10.6oz)
★Butter dough ....150g / 5.29oz
♥Cake flour ....108g / 3.81oz
  Almond flour....................21g / 0.74oz
  Purple sweet potato powder................
  ....21g / 0.74oz

●Yellow: Pumpkin (about 200g / 7.05oz)
★Butter dough ....100g / 3.53oz
♥Cake flour ....72g / 2.54oz
  Almond flour.....................14g / 0.49oz
  Pumpkin powder.............14g / 0.49oz

* Depending on the person who makes it, the size
of the parts may vary so the amounts for the
ingredients are on the generous side.

24

STOCKING

MAKE THE BASIC PARTS

*All parts are 8cm (3.1in) in length.

STRIPE PATTERN
Four sheets of purple
sweet potato dough (room
temperature) 4cm (1.6in) wide
and 1cm (0.4in) thick, and five
sheets of pumpkin dough (room
temperature) 4cm (1.6in) wide
and 1cm (0.4in) thick.

METHOD

1 Use the ★ ingredients to make the butter dough. (See p. 64.)
2 Add the ♥ ingredients to make up the two different colored doughs.

1

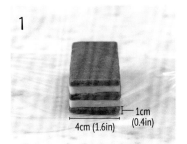

Make four sheets of purple sweet potato dough and five sheets of pumpkin dough (room temperature). Layer three sheets of the purple sweet potato dough and two sheets of the pumpkin dough alternately. Ensure they are all stuck together.
⇒Freeze for 15 mins.

2

Layer a sheet of purple sweet potato dough and pumpkin dough left over from step 1. On top of that place a semi-cylindrical piece of purple sweet potato dough (frozen). Ensure everything sticks together.
⇒Freeze for 5 mins.

3

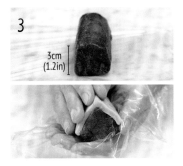

Make a fan-shaped piece of purple sweet potato dough (frozen) with the straight side measuring 3cm (1.2in). Use the last two sheets of pumpkin dough to cover the straight sides of the fan-shaped piece of dough.

4

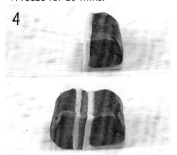

Attach step 3 to step 2 firmly and ensure everything sticks together.

5

Turn step 4 upside down and fix up the shape.
⇒Freeze for 15–20 mins.

FINISHED STOCKING

Attach step 1 to step 5 firmly. The Stocking is finished after ensuring everything sticks together.
⇒Freeze for 30 mins or longer.

Cut into 0.7–0.8cm (0.3in) thick slices and bake for 15 mins in an oven preheated to 170°C/338°F, then lower the temperature to 160°C/320°F and finish by baking for another 5–8 mins.

INGREDIENTS

★Butter dough (about 140g / 4.94oz)
Unsalted butter...............70g / 2.47oz
Powdered sugar ....53g / 1.87oz
Whole egg.........................18g / 0.63oz
1 pinch of salt

●Green: Matcha (about 105g / 3.7oz)
★Butter dough ....53g / 1.87oz
♥Cake flour ....39g / 1.38oz
Almond flour......................7g / 0.25oz
Matcha powder ....6g / 0.21oz

●White: Plain (about 80g / 2.82oz)
★Butter dough ....40g / 1.41oz
♥Cake flour ....33g / 1.16oz
Almond flour......................7g / 0.25oz

* Depending on the person who makes it, the size
of the parts may vary so the amounts for the
ingredients are on the generous side.

25

CHRISTMAS TREE

MAKE THE BASIC PARTS   *All parts are 8cm (3.1in) in length.

TRUNK
A square-shaped piece of cocoa dough
(room temperature) measuring 2cm
(0.8in) wide and 1cm (0.4in) thick.

● Red: Raspberry (about 65g / 2.29oz)	● Brown: Cocoa (about 20g / 0.71oz)
★ Butter dough ....33g / 1.16oz	★ Butter dough ....10g / 0.35oz
♥ Cake flour ....24g / 0.85oz	♥ Cake flour ....7g / 0.25oz
Almond flour......................5g / 0.18oz	Almond flour......................2g / 0.07oz
Raspberry powder ....4g / 0.14oz	Cocoa powder ....2g / 0.07oz

METHOD

1. Use the ★ ingredients to make the butter dough. (See p. 64.)
2. Add the ♥ ingredients to make up the four different colored doughs.

1

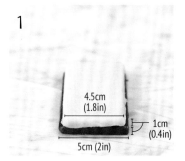

Place a sheet of plain dough (room temperature) 4.5cm (1.8in) wide and 1cm (0.4in) thick on top of a sheet of matcha dough (room temperature) measuring 5cm (2in) wide and 1cm (0.4in) thick.

2

On top of step 1, place a sheet of raspberry dough (room temperature) 4cm (1.6in) wide and 1cm (0.4in) thick, and a sheet of matcha dough (room temperature) 3.5cm (1.4in) wide and 1cm (0.4in) thick.

3

On top of step 2, place a sheet of plain dough (room temperature) 3cm (1.2in) wide and 1cm (0.4in) thick, and a sheet of raspberry dough (room temperature) 2.5cm (1in) wide and 1cm (0.4in) thick.

4

On top of step 3, place a sheet of matcha dough (room temperature) 2cm (0.8in) wide and 1cm (0.4in) thick. Fix up the overall shape.
⇒Freeze for 15–20 mins.

5

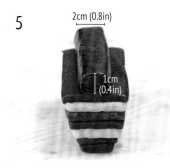

Turn step 4 upside down and attach a square-shaped piece of cocoa dough (room temperature) measuring 2cm (0.8in) wide and 1cm (0.4in) thick.
⇒Freeze for 5 mins.

FINISHED CHRISTMAS TREE

Ensure step 5 is attached firmly and everything is stuck together. The Christmas Tree is finished after fixing up the overall shape.
⇒Freeze for 30 mins or longer.

Cut into 0.7–0.8cm (0.3in) thick slices and bake for 15 mins in an oven preheated to 170°C/338°F, then lower the temperature to 160°C/320°F and finish by baking for another 5 mins.

Planning: Emi Nihei

Editors: Hanae Soga, Ryotaro Shiba (Fig Inc)

Design: Kyoko Hirama (Studio Dunk)

Illustrations: Natsuko Komuten

Drawing: Chieko Takahashi

Photography: Mai Ichise (Studio Dunk), Yuki Miwa

Stylist: Yukari Kimura

Ingredients Supplier: cotta (http://www.cotta.co.jp/)

Photography Support: UTUWA (Myojo Building 1F, 3-50-11 Sendagaya, Shibuya-ku, Tokyo 150-0051)

Translation: Victoria Oyama
Thanks to TIME & SPACE, INC. for help with translation

Aiko Kawamura (Minotake Seika)

Born in Fujisawa, Kanagawa Prefecture, Japan. While working as a magazine editor, she aspired to become an editor specializing in food. After studying French style cuisine courses and patisserie courses at Le Cordon Bleu's culinary school in Tokyo, she attained the Grand Diplome qualification. Since 2012, under the trade name of Minotake Seika, Kawamura has been selling her baked products made with the ingredients that she herself likes, at events such as markets for handmade products.

English edition published in 2019 by:

NIPPAN IPS Co., Ltd.

1-3-4 Yushima

Bunkyo-ku, Tokyo,

113-0034 Japan

ISBN 978-4-86505-225-1

Minotakeseika no Icebox Cookie

©2015,minotakeseika.

Original Japanese edition is published by Seibundo Shinkosha Publishing Co., Ltd.

Printed in China